Dressmaking with Basic Patterns

Dressmaking with Basic Patterns

Ann Ladbury

B.T. Batsford Limited *London*

Filmset by Servis Filmsetting Ltd, Manchester
Printed in Great Britain by litho at The Anchor Press Ltd
and bound by Wm Brendon & Son Ltd
both of Tiptree, Essex

ISBN 0 7134 3850 9

Contents

SECTION I

PATTERNS AND PATTERN ADJUSTMENTS

I

Introduction

Although I have never been taught tailoring, I have probably absorbed some of it through it being around at home and through watching my father, and also because it has been in the family for several generations. It is probably because of this that I seem always to have applied something of tailoring techniques to dressmaking to achieve, I think, more professional looking results. The methods described in this book are those I have used myself for years but they have also been well tested by many students, both when I was teaching, and more recently by television viewers and people attending residential courses. This doesn't mean that I am still using and teaching the same things; on the contrary I am constantly revising what I do in order to cope with new fabrics and to incorporate new products (not gimmicks!). For example, those of you who have my earlier books, written several years ago, will see that I have developed a different approach to tailoring trousers and have discovered even more fitting problems.

In making my own clothes I have evolved better methods which students have also found easier to manage, thereby achieving more satisfying results.

This book contains basic dress and trouser patterns for 83–97cm (32in.–38in.) bust sizes. There are diagram-patterns for you to copy on to sheets of squared paper. If you don't wish to scale up these diagrams you can buy a basic dress and trouser pattern and use them in conjunction with this book.

The early sections in the book cover the fitting and adjusting of the patterns and instructions on the processes needed for making them up.

The last section contains a few simple adaptations, including converting the two-piece dress pattern into one without a waist join.

This is not intended as a course on pattern drafting, but gives a few ideas on how you can easily change the style but still use the same pattern.

2

Using basic patterns

The great advantage of using a basic pattern is that the adjustments for your figure problems are already done, leaving only the fitting in fabric to be done. For those with more than one figure problem, this saves time, ensures an accurate start and also – possibly the most important reason – it ensures that the adjustments are made properly and not skimped or omitted altogether. Most of us hanker after the perfect shape and perhaps sometimes imagine that we have it. It is surprising the number of women who, after perhaps years of adjusting their pattern, will quite suddenly slap a pattern on the fabric and cut out without alteration. They can offer no explanation for the lapse except that they knew while they were doing it that it wasn't going to work, or that because it was that particular style

they didn't think it would matter. We don't magically acquire perfect proportions overnight and so a basic pattern, altered and ready for use is a help.

A basic dress pattern can be made up in different fabrics to produce a variety of effects, but in addition, the pattern can be adapted endlessly to make garments that are quite different in appearance but retain the same basic elements of fit.

Trousers, fortunately, cannot change much except in leg width, and as the fitting problems are so much more tricky it is a great relief to most people to have an adjusted basic pattern.

From these two patterns, the dress and trousers, you can produce many of the outfits you need.

3

Basic dress

Description

A waisted dress with A-line skirt, slit neckline and slim sleeve. The bodice front is shaped with an underarm dart and a waist dart, the back with a waist dart and a neck dart. The centre front and centre back seams are straight, although they can be adjusted at fitting to introduce more shaping if necessary. There is a centre back zip, and a basic neckline and armhole. The sleeve is shaped with a single elbow dart and the wrist is wide enough for the hand to slip through without an opening. The waistline has a petersham stay sewn in but this can be omitted by those who prefer to be without its firm feel.

The sleeve head and armhole have been shaped to give a fairly straight back armhole and therefore more ease of movement, reducing the risk of splitting, and the front is scooped out to give a smooth fit. The lowest point of the armhole is not at the underarm seam, but, for comfort, a little to the front. The sleeve head is not too deep and the shoulder seam is short. There are many, many women with sloping, narrow, shoulders and sloping top arm, and it is easier to add on for the broader ones. Finally, there are two positions where a high, close fit are essential for freedom of movement and therefore comfort: one is the crutch point (explained in the first section on trousers), and the other is under the arm so that you can raise your arms without the whole dress lifting. The armhole, therefore, is high but carefully shaped so that it is not tight. Nothing is more uncomfortable than a low armhole.

3.1 Choosing the pattern size

On the whole, you use the pattern nearest to your bust size because with the checking that comes later, and the fitting, the other areas can be corrected. Also, it is easier to adjust the hips, by taking in or letting out the seams, than it is to alter the bust size. If, however, your bust and hips are excessively out of proportion, it would be easier to choose the smaller pattern and make it larger where neeed. The size of your frame may help you to decide, and also whether you have a particular figure problem, or one area that is out of proportion. Length is relatively unimportant at this stage because it is easy to adjust and also, as you will see, we have to consider the proportional length of each part of the body before finally establishing such things as skirt and sleeve length.

However, here are some examples of figure types and what people should consider when deciding which pattern to use. These points also apply if you fall between sizes.
(i) A tall well-built woman with a small bust, but otherwise relatively in proportion, should choose a large pattern which fits her everywhere except at the bust, and reduce the bust dart before she begins.
(ii) A petite woman with small bones but with one area out of proportion, for example, a prominent D cup bust, should start with the small pattern and enlarge the bust dart and front length.
(iii) The pear-shaped person, as a general rule,

will fare best with the pattern that fits her bust, especially if her waist and rib cage are small and her arms are short, as is often the case, because she can alter for her hips or thighs without too much trouble.

(iv)   The person with a narrow back, narrow shoulders and chest, thin arms and small armholes, but large low bust and thick waist (and possibly very slim hips and flat bottom) should use a small size pattern because the subtle curves at neck and armhole are more difficult to adjust than the bust and waist.

3.2 Making your pattern

'True Sew' squared paper, pencil, tape measure, ruler, rubber, paper scissors.

Copy your size pattern onto squared paper, following the diagram. Mark turnings 1·5cm ($\frac{5}{8}$in.) all round and 5cm (2in.) at the hem. The quickest way to do this is to use a measuring gauge of the type produced by Milward's, or cut a marker from a piece of cardboard, with 1·5cm ($\frac{5}{8}$in.) carefully measured along one edge. Mark centre front and centre back on all pieces and also the straight grain lines and bust point. Label each pattern piece 'back', 'front', etc.

Making pattern

5/8 in marker

Checking the size of your pattern

You will already be aware of some of the differences between your own measurements and those of the pattern so the pattern should be checked and altered at this stage before cutting out. When you use a pattern for the first time, particularly a basic one which you will want to be very accurate and reliable, you cannot expect to

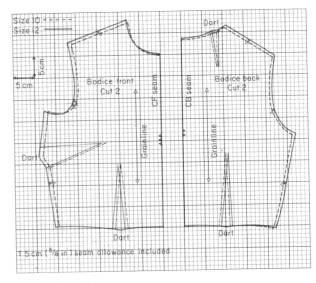

Basic dress sizes 10–12

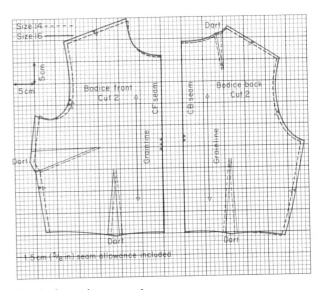

Basic dress sizes 14–16

correct everything at the paper stage. Other points will reveal themselves when you try the garment on in fabric, and you will then record those on the pattern.

Some measurements can be checked by pinning the pattern on to the body but others are best checked by measuring the figure and working

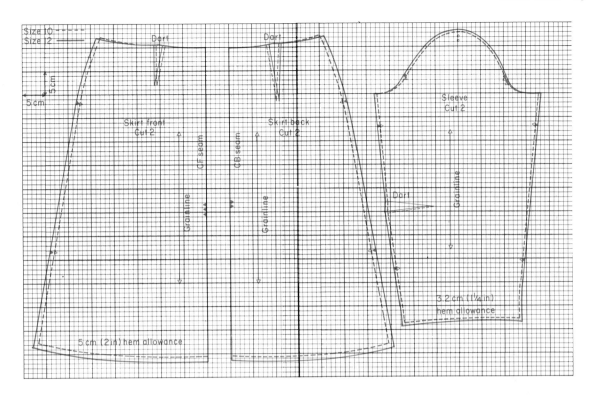

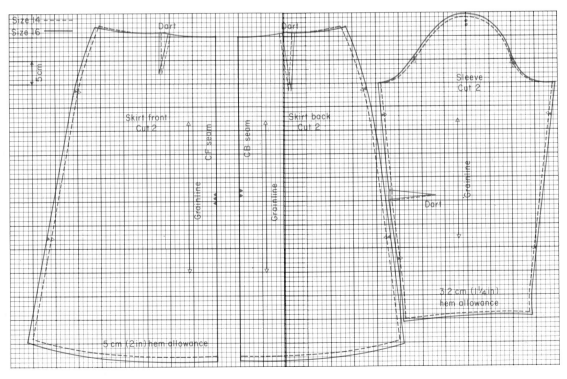

*1   Tracing-off a diagram pattern (courtesy
H.W. Peel & Co)*

with the pattern flat on the table. To all measurements add 6mm ($\frac{1}{4}$in.) ease and measure within
the pattern, omitting the turnings.

(i) Depth of armhole
You may have found the standard armhole too
low, or, occasionally, too high for you. The armhole in this pattern, which is a sloping egg-shape
rather than horse shoe, should be more comfortable but check the depth on the pattern. Draw a
line (Fig. 1a) from the lowest point of the underarm back across to the centre back, at right angles
to the centre back. Slide a ruler under your arm
and hold it horizontally while someone measures
from centre back of neck down to edge of ruler
and compare with the depth on the pattern. Pin
the back and front patterns together at underarm

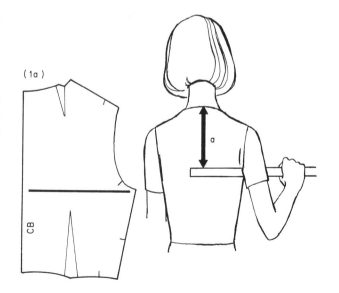

shoulder seam a little. It is best not to do this on the pattern because it is by no means always correct on every figure. The sleeve remains unaltered, you would only need to enlarge or reduce the sleeve head if you made a massive alteration to the depth of armhole. Now the armhole depth has been altered, the back and front bodice pieces are different lengths so make the next check which will correct it.

(ii) Centre back and centre front length
Measure from top spinal bone down back to waist and from hollow of neck at front down to waist (Fig. 2a). Check the pattern and lengthen or shorten by pleating or cutting just above the waist (Figs. 2b&c). Note that if waist line is uneven this may well be an uneven alteration.

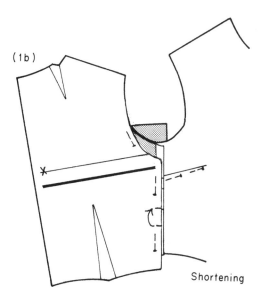

(1b)

Shortening

(Fig. 1b) and measure. If the armhole on the pattern is too deep, move the back pattern down, so shortening the distance between neck and underarm point. Fill in back armhole curve to make a good line with the front armhole. If the armhole is too shallow, move the back pattern up (Fig. 1c) and cut out the back armhole curve.

Mark a new balance mark across the two patterns, at the side seam, before unpinning. Having altered the back armhole, be prepared, at the fitting stage, to raise or lower the front

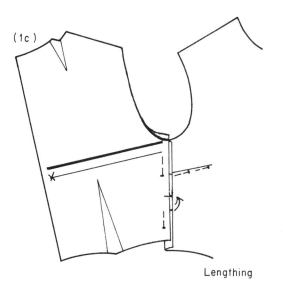

(1c)

Lengthing

(2a)

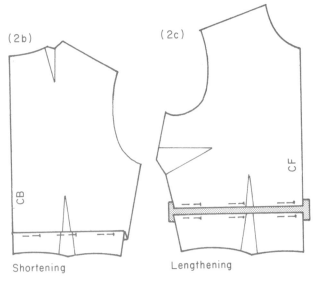

(2b)   (2c)

CB

CF

Shortening   Lengthening

(iv) Depth of bust point

Measure from centre of shoulder line down to point of bust.

To lower the bust point (Fig. 4a), pleat the paper below the level of the bust dart, taking out the necessary amount, pin or stick. Cut the pattern across above the dart, but below the arm-hole and insert the same amount. Re-measure before sticking down. Shorten the waist dart to correspond.

To raise the bust point, do the same thing (Fig. 4b), but pleating above the dart and cutting below, or, if the adjustment is less than 1.3cm ($\frac{1}{2}$in.) simply re-draw the dart from the same

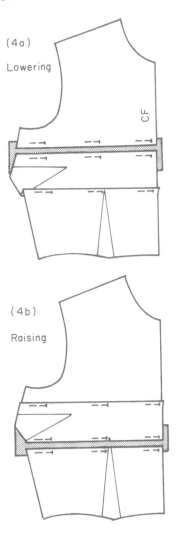

(4a)

Lowering

CF

(4b)

Raising

(iii) Back neck width

Stand your tape measure on edge and measure round the curve from centre back to shoulder seam, missing out the neck dart. If you need the neck wider (Fig. 3a), raise the point where the neck and shoulder seam meet and re-draw the shoulder seam and neck curve. If the neck is too wide for you (Fig. 3b), mark off your own measurement on the neck curve and from that point re-draw the shoulder seam. It is best to leave the front neck until the fitting stage because it is easier to look at the effect of the neckline on you rather than to try to do it by measuring. Again, too, correcting the back neck often puts the front one right as well.

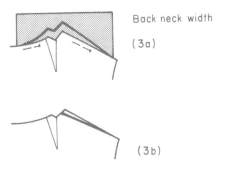

Back neck width

(3a)

(3b)

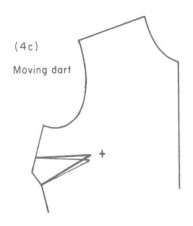

(4c)

Moving dart

base but to a higher point (Fig. 4c). *Note*: The bust dart should end 1·3cm (½in.) short of the actual bust point, or the garment will feel tight.

(v) Check for prominent bust

Measure from middle of shoulder line down over bust prominence to waist. Check this length on the pattern. To lengthen for prominent bust cut through dart to the point and from there to the centre front. Open the two pieces inserting extra paper to give the required length. Pin or stick in position. Re-draw the bust dart from the same base points but running to a new point 1·3cm (½in.) from the bust point cross (Fig. 5). *Note*: If the pattern seems too long when you check for

prominent bust, do not shorten it at this stage, you will not know whether the excess is above or below the armhole.

(vi) Shoulder length

This is a difficult measurement to check accurately because if the back is particularly rounded or fleshy it might be necessary to have a slightly longer shoulder seam. However, measure the pattern and adjust as follows if necessary.

Cut the pattern from the centre of the shoulder seam down to the middle of the armhole, almost to the edge of the paper. Shorten the shoulder by overlapping the two cut edges (Fig. 6a), or lengthen by opening them out (Fig. 6b). Pin down, then re-draw a straight shoulder seam from neck to shoulder. Alter back and front in the same way.

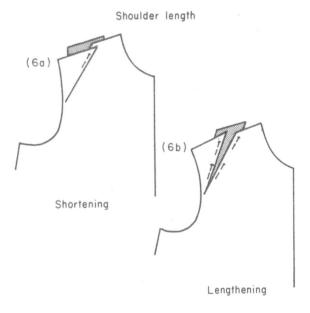

Shoulder length

(6a)

(6b)

Shortening

Lengthening

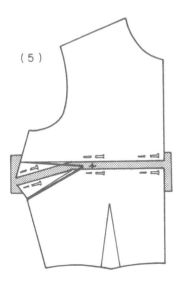

(5)

(vii) Sleeve width

Measure round muscular part of top arm, below armhole, add 2·5cm (1in.) for ease and check the width of the pattern at this level. If it seems that the sleeve may be tight, cut the pattern down the centre from head to wrist, but leave 6mm (¼in.) attached each end. Cut across the sleeve

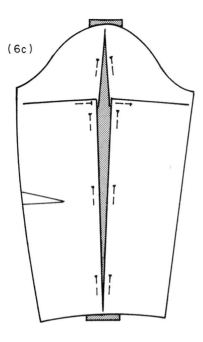

(6c)

too, leaving it joined at the edges. Put the pattern onto a strip of paper or Vilene and part the two sections, inserting some additional width (Fig. 6c). Keep all four sections flat and pin down.

(viii) Sleeve length

The precise finished length will depend on the fabric but adjust the pattern to approximately the right length before cutting out. The most accurate place to measure is the underarm seam so measure a garment you have and check the pattern. Make a note of any adjustment to be made but wait until you have tried on the pattern before deciding where to alter it. This is described under Checking the Pattern on the Body, the next section.

3.3 Taking your measurements

It seems to me that the 'average' woman is no-where to be found, or at least that she is quite content with an off-the-peg wardrobe, for I have never met her. We have to accept that we come in all shapes and sizes and in order to achieve a good fit we must first find out exactly where we deviate from this mythical 'average'. Having discovered your peculiarities, often, I am afraid, only by first making a number of garments that don't fit, you then set about learning how and where to alter the pattern at those points, and how to fit in fabric to cope with problems of posture and to establish width and length.

To take your measurements successfully you really need the assistance of someone else so that you can simply stand still. Also, if two or more of you are involved, by taking each other's measurements you will learn a lot about figure types and body proportion just by comparing your sizes with your appearance. For instance, it might well be that three of you all measure 92cm (36in.) bust, but if you stand together your busts will all be at different heights and they will be different sizes, your waists will be at different levels, hands hanging at different points (important when positioning pockets) and also your knees will vary in position. Stand sideways and you will probably be horrified at your postures too, some backs will be long, some short. And yet, of course, you will probably use the same pattern and expect it to fit you.

Wear a thin jumper with set in sleeves and a skirt or trousers. You need certain lines such as armhole, neck and waist to be defined and if you strip to foundation garments all guide lines are lost. Even if you wear something you don't consider is a good fit at these points it will be obvious where the line ought to be and it is easy enough to measure, for instance, back neck-to-waist length and add a little on if you are aware that what you are wearing is too short in the waist.

The measurements listed in a later section will be needed for checking the pattern before cutting out in fabric, but to help you decide which size pattern to draw, you need to know the following:
(i)   Bust: run tape round fullest part of bust, under the arms (1). The tape should meet comfortably.
(ii) Hips: run tape round fullest part of hips. This is where the actual hip bone sticks out most (2); do not measure round buttocks unless they are at hip level, and do not measure thighs.

Figure types

Taking
measurements

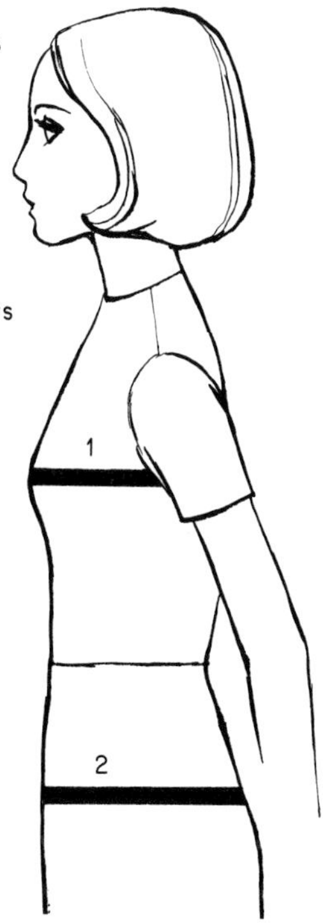

(I)

Remember that the figures you write down are only a guide, the amount of ease you need for movement varies a lot depending on whether you are energetic, how much muscle and fat there is, and sometimes on what you do for a living. Women who do a lot of manual work, for example, need a great deal of shoulder and sleeve ease! The precise amount of ease can only be determined later when the garment is tried on, and it will vary with each fabric you use. Make a chart for future reference, as shown here.

MEASUREMENTS

	Pattern	Mine	Pattern	Mine	Pattern	Mine	Pattern	Mine	Pattern	Mine
1 Bust	87 (34)		92 (36)		97 (38)		102 (40)		107 (42)	
2 Hips	92 (36)		97 (38)		102 (40)		107 (42)		112 (44)	
3 Waist										
4 Depth of armhole										
5 C.B. length										
6 C.F. length										
7 Back neck width										
8 Depth of bust point										
9 Shoulder length										
10 Sleeve seam length										

(Figures in brackets indicate inches)

3.4 Mounting basic patterns

Having checked and altered a basic pattern, it is a good idea to make a more durable copy of it for future use.

Those pattern pieces that have not been extensively altered you can support with light-weight iron-on Vilene as follows:
Place each piece, right side up, onto the wrong side of the Vilene, ie. the side covered with shiny granules; anchor with a pin. Using a warm iron but no moisture, press the central area of each piece until it sticks to the Vilene. Take care not to put your iron on the Vilene alone. Trim round each pattern piece carefully, making sure you cut accurately, and leaving the necessary turnings. Run the iron over each piece again, this time also pressing the edges. Any simple alterations to the paper pattern such as pleats for shortening, will be kept in place by the Vilene backing.

If your original paper pattern is badly mutilated by alterations it would be as well to make a new pattern from Vilene. Use a lightweight sew-in grade, not an iron-on grade. Place the pattern underneath the Vilene, anchor with pins and trace the pattern and all markings, using a felt pen and ruler. Cut out each piece carefully.

Store your basic pattern in a large labelled envelope: it will be usable for a long time. Keep your altered paper pattern in it and put the date on, as it will serve as a useful reminder in the future as to exactly what you had to do at that time.

You could, of course, delay making the more durable pattern until after the dress has been made up, in case further alterations become necessary.

3.5 Preparation of pattern

Having adjusted it and if necessary cut a new one in Vilene, your pattern should be ready for use. Make sure such things as grain line and 'fold' are marked where necessary. Run a warm iron over the pieces to smooth out creases.

Cut out only the main body sections and the sleeve. Do not cut facings, collars, or other small pieces until after fitting. At this stage simply reserve a place for them on your length of fabric, dovetailing them in with the bigger pieces but then removing them before pinning.

3.6 Figure types

Basic dress, round neck, slit opening. CF seam, waist seam, long sleeve semi-fitted and CB zip

This basic dress will suit most figures and it is a useful item in the wardrobe. If you haven't worn a waisted dress for years, try this one, it isn't tight fitting and will not have the effect of cutting you in half, and it has a slimming centre seam. If you are adamant that you cannot have a waist join at all, make this up in calico or old sheeting in order to conquer the problems of fit and then go on to convert it to a one-piece pattern.

3.7 Applying measurements

Checking the pattern by pinning on the body
Having fitted so many people, both while I was teaching, and in recent years, at residential courses, I have found it more successful to confine adjustments on the body to those of balance; that is, length, and leave the question of precise width until the garment is fitted in fabric.

Alterations with the pattern pinned to you
It is difficult to fit in paper because it is unyielding and it tears. In fact I normally cut a basic pattern in lightweight Vilene for this but you may prefer to delay that until you can incorporate all your alterations, particularly if you are not yet sure how extensive they are going to be.

Having adjusted the pattern as far as possible you can now pin it on to the body to check the length of each piece.

Marking horizontal lines
To help position the pieces correctly, mark the following lines:
(i)   On front skirt, draw a line at right angles to the centre front seam, 20cm (8in.) below the waist; mark this 'hip line'. (Fig. 1.)
(ii)   On the sleeve, draw two lines straight across; one through the point of the elbow dart and one at the underarm. (Fig. 2.)
(iii)   On the front bodice draw a line (Fig. 3) through the bust point at right angles to the centre front seam. Draw another from the base of the neck to the armhole.

Fitting the pattern for length
Imagine a number of horizontal lines running round your body at various levels; it is at these places that we are going to compare the pattern

(1)

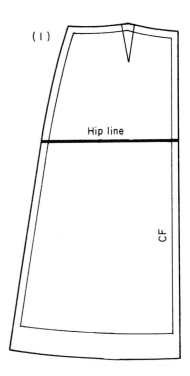

Hip line

CF

(2)

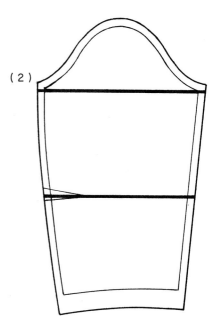

(3)

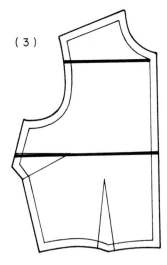

(4)

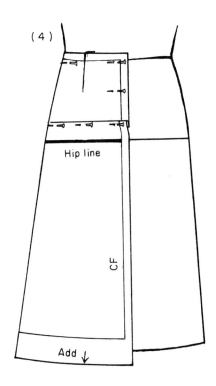

Hip line

CF

Add ↓

length with the actual figure. Adjusting these now by shortening or lengthening the pattern will ensure that the balance is correct for the figure and will make the first fitting of the dress much easier.

As you pin each piece into position see whether the width at bust, waist, hips and thighs is sufficient. As you are wearing clothes the edges of the paper should meet at the side seams. The width fitting can only be done accurately when you try on the fabric so at this stage simply make sure the pattern is large enough. If it seems doubtful make a note on the pattern to remind you to add more when you cut out.

Hip line

Pin front skirt to person at centre front at waist and again a little below. Smooth pattern round figure and pin at side waist.

Check position of hip line on the pattern when joined to the figure. The hip level is not the seat, thighs, or even buttocks, but it is the point at which the hip bone protrudes most, at the side of the figure (Fig. 4). It is from this level that a skirt should swing. On many women I have fitted, we have discovered hip bones as little as 10 or 12cm (4 or 5in.) below the waist. I have had to raise the hipline on all but a handful of the

thousands of people I have fitted, and I have never come across anyone who needed it lowered. It is even necessary to raise it on tall women if their hip bone is high. In fact, it seems to happen that the shorter than average woman often has short legs and a lower hip than the tall, long-legged one!

The buttocks and stomach are fitted by darts, the thighs are fitted by extra width but are also disguised by style, but putting the hip line right before you start ensures a good hang and an attractive swing rather than a droopy caved-in look.

Pleat up the pattern to bring the line into position and pin. Before removing pattern, check skirt length, allowing for the hem. If skirt is too short, make a note on the pattern to cut longer by adding to the hemline. If too long, the exact length will be established later in fabric, and then recorded on the pattern.

Remove pattern piece and smooth the pleat across. Pin or stick. Place back skirt pattern beside it and make the same alteration.

Bust line and waist line

Pin pattern pieces to the front with horizontal lines in position and check the length. In spite of your flat measurements, you may find surplus length to be pleated out or a shortness which indicates that the pattern has to be cut across at that point and extra length put in. Check at the centre front, side seam, centre back and shoulder seam.

Alterations that may be needed are:

(i) Shorten bodice

Pleat on the figure to bring waistline into position, it may not be a level pleat all round. (Fig. 5.)

(5)

Shortening

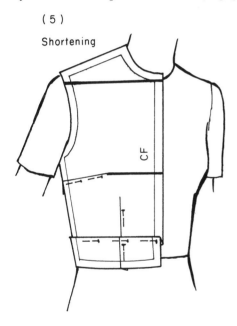

(ii) Lengthen bodice

Unpin the lower edge, cut pattern across from centre front round to centre back about 5cm (2in.) above waist, drop lower sections and pin in place. Insert extra paper in the space. (Fig. 6.)

(iii) Lengthen at centre back

This is often needed by the elderly or those who work in a stooping position. Pin the bodice in position at the underarm and pin the horizontal line across the back. Smooth pattern up to neck.

(6)

Lengthening

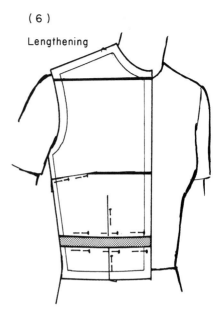

If it seems short, cut pattern across halfway down armhole and open up at centre back only, pin extra paper in the gap. When cutting out, the centre back seam should be straightened although it may be necessary to shape it a little when it comes to fitting. The neck dart may have to be made a little bigger but leave this too until fitting. (Fig. 7a&b.)

(7a)

CB length

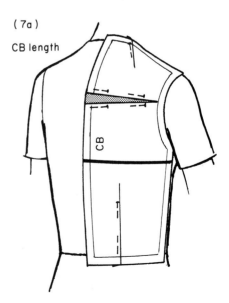

(7b)

Straight
CB seam

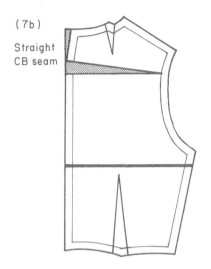

little at the neck point (Figs. 8a&b). If the previous alteration for the rounded back has been done this automatically lifts the neck point and if the shoulders are also sloping then the trouble may be corrected.

(v) Sleeve length

Pin dart and pin sleeve seams and slip onto bare arm. Bend elbow slightly and check position of elbow dart. This should be a little below the actual elbow (Fig. 9). If the sleeve needs lengthening or shortening above or below the elbow, or, in both positions, take off and unpin and adjust.

There are two width problems that might reveal themselves while the pattern is pinned to the body. One is chest width and the other is back width, and the two sometimes go together.

(iv) Shoulders

With very square or very sloping shoulders you may need to add extra before cutting out. For square shoulders pin extra paper and raise the shoulder edge (Fig. 8a). For sloping shoulders, fold away at shoulder edge and possibly add a

(9)

Sleeve length

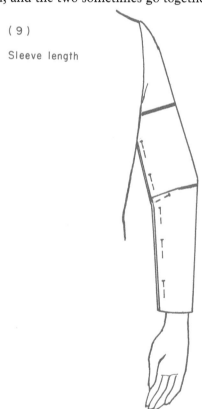

(8a)

Shoulders

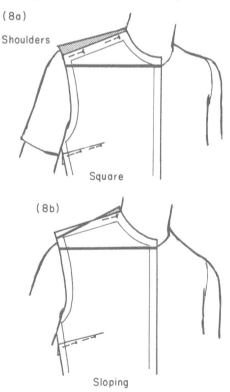

Square

(8b)

Sloping

Chest width

If there seems to be surplus paper between neck and armhole, or if you know from experience that you are narrow chested, try folding back the edge of the pattern at the neck, running it to nothing at the waist. In addition it is quite likely that you will have to reduce the length by pleating out a small amount between neck and armhole. (Fig. 10.)

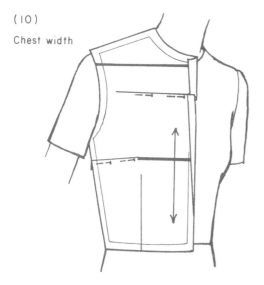

(10)

Chest width

Back width

If the pattern seems tight across the armholes, then extra must be allowed. A little can be added to centre back when cutting out, then used if necessary, or if the tightness is at the armhole only, then some extra can be added at the armhole edge. If the problem is severe the pattern should be cut down from neck point to waist and opened out. (Figs. 11a&b.)

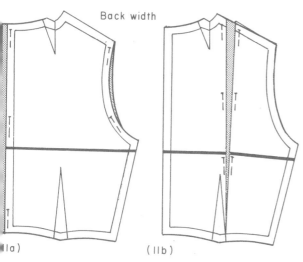

Back width

(11a)   (11b)

3.8 Correcting pattern edges

Whenever you make a pattern alteration you are likely to disturb the smooth run of the pattern edge. This can be serious if not corrected, especially where darts are concerned, as you may find a gap when you come to stitch up the nearby seam.

(i) Lengthening a pattern
After inserting extra paper and pinning it or sticking it in place, draw in straight lines with a ruler, curved edges should be filled in with a gentle hand-drawn curve (Fig. 1). Trim off surplus paper.

(ii) Shortening a pattern
This creates a step which must be smoothed out by adding a little to one edge and taking a little off the other edge. If the seam is straight (Fig. 2), place a ruler along the main part of the seam and draw a line across the folded paper. Trim off surplus paper. If the seam is shaped (Fig. 2), draw a freehand curve following the general run of the seam. Trim off surplus paper.

(1)   (2)

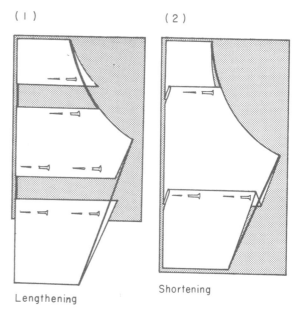

Lengthening   Shortening

(iii) Shortened or lengthened darts
Use a ruler to draw new lines from the base of the
dart to the point. (Figs. 3a&b.)

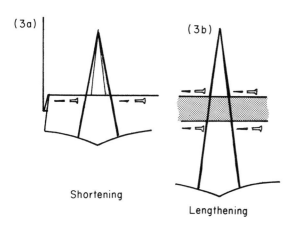

Shortening

Lengthening

(iv) Darts moved or altered in size
Pin extra paper under the edge of the pattern
(Fig. 4a). Fold the dart and press it to one side in
the direction it will go when sewn and finished
(Fig. 4b); that is, bust darts downwards, all
others towards centre front or centre back. Pin
dart down firmly and cut along line of seam to

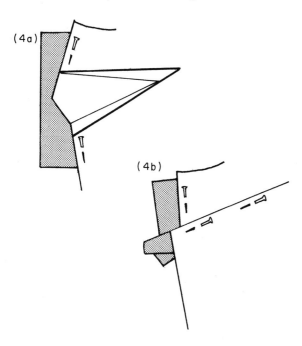

remove surplus paper. If the paper is springy
you can draw a line first as a guide but you must
still cut with the paper folded. Unpin the dart
and open out and you will see that the end of the
dart is now shaped. (Fig. 4c.)

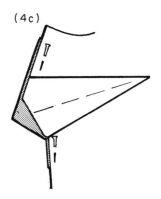

3.9 Preparation of fabric

Some fabrics need special preparation and these
are dealt with in later sections where their
suggested use is discussed. All fabrics need the
following preparation.

Grain

(i) Grain on plain woven fabric
Although the warp threads, which run the length
of the fabric, are parallel with the selvedge and
are therefore straight, the weft threads running
across the width may not necessarily be at right
angles to them. Sometimes, in finishing the
material is pulled and is then folded and rolled
up, thereby holding the weft threads crooked.
Sometimes too it is cut crookedly in the shop.
Straighten the end by lifting up one thread with a
pin and easing it out. There is no need to pull the
thread right out, if you simply disturb it a little
right across it will leave a mark as you will know
only too well from accidental snagging. (Fig. 1a.)

If the material is badly off grain don't cut off the
triangle that appears, just in case you find you
need it for cutting out a small piece of the garment.
This is another good reason for not actually
removing the thread, this piece can always be

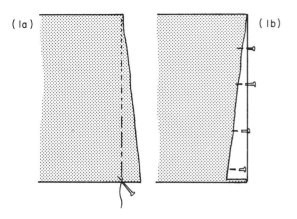

incorporated in the hem. Fold the fabric so that the marker thread is lying level and put in a few pins. (Fig. 1b.)

Smooth out the rest of the fabric to see if it will lie flat with the selvedges together. If not, then the weft threads are indeed off true and you should get someone to help you to pull them straight. Open out the fabric and take the two shorter corners opposite. Pull and pull like a tug of war until the fabric does lie flat on the table. (Fig. 1c.)

Pin the end, pin the selvedges and press, to settle the threads in their new position. You may need to use a damp cloth or at least a steam iron to smooth out the bubbles. (Fig. 1d.)

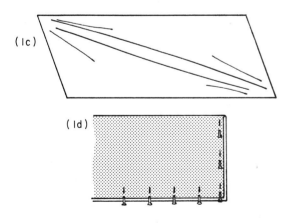

(ii) Grain on plain jersey fabrics

Using tailor's chalk and a ruler, draw a line across the fabric following a line of knitting. This can be difficult to see but it is the same construction as hand knitting. Fold and pin to check that it will lie flat. Synthetic jersey is almost impossible to straighten by pulling but you can usually ensure a straight grain on each piece of garment by folding the end level and smoothing a small area, lay on a pattern piece and cut, re-line the grain, smooth out and cut another piece, and so on.

With bonded fabrics the backing fabric is unlikely to be following the same grain as the top fabric, so be sure to straighten, fold and cut out following the right side only.

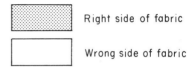

Right side of fabric

Wrong side of fabric

Shrinkage

Most finishing now includes shrinkage so it is unlikely that you will encounter this problem on any fabric that has a manufacturer's name on it. However, all fabric is woven or knitted, of necessity, under tension and sometimes with loosely woven material and even some knitteds, immersing in water for the first time has the effect of releasing the tension and causing the fibres to close up. The length of fibre remains the same so this is not shrinkage as we used to know it. Even a Crimplene dress, plunged for its first wash into an automatic machine on hot wash, and left to spin relentlessly at the end will suffer this closing up. Even in these days of wanting to wash everything in this way you can avoid this trouble by washing gently by hand and drip-drying, and also pressing, in the early part of the garment's life, and anyway surely it does deserve a little more care when new than sheets, shirts and socks, especially when you have made it yourself.

If you have bought an unlabelled length from a market stall, if your fabric was abnormally cheap, or if you are at all doubtful about its future behaviour, test it for shrinkage. Measure out a 15cm (6in.) square somewhere in the middle of the length and mark it with tacking if it is a fabric you will be washing, or chalk it if it is to be a

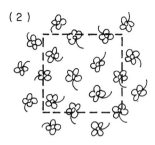

garment you will only have cleaned (Fig. 2). Then wash this area, or press it with a damp muslin. Allow it to dry, press it and re-measure it both ways. If there is any change then tack the ends and selvedge together and wash or damp press the whole piece.

Incidentally, if you are using synthetic jersey and you are prone to the effects of a build up of static electricity, wash the whole length in a fabric softener such as Comfort before cutting out.

(iii) One way fabrics

Most patterned fabrics except for even designs such as gingham have to be cut one-way and these are referred to in a later section. Plain woven fabrics can be cut with pieces lying in both directions, but any knitted fabric should be cut as a one-way material. The construction of the knitting, means that the loops all lie in one direction as with hand knitting and this can cause a slight shading, especially if the fibre is shiny. With some knitted fabric it will be obvious that it is one-way.

3.10 Interfacing

Certain areas of all garments need reinforcing to prevent them losing their shape in the course of wear. The type of interfacing used is a matter of individual choice and availability, but the weight is very important. If it is too heavy it will show because that part of the garment will appear different; if it is too light it will be ineffective.

Specific types and grades of interfacing are

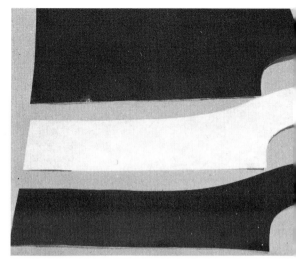

2   *Cutting interfacing (courtesy Vilene Ltd)*

detailed for each fabric suggested in the book, and instructions for how to use it and where to put it are included for each garment.

Bondina-Vilene Ltd make a range of non-woven interfacings which are widely available and their recommendations are shown in the table opposite.

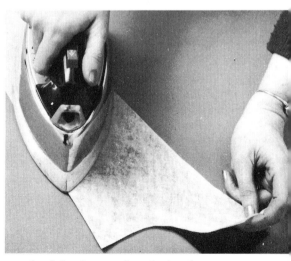

3   *Applying iron-on interfacing (courtesy Vilene Ltd)*

CHOOSING THE CORRECT INTERFACING

SEW-IN VILENE

Weight	*Suitable for :*	*Washing*	*Dry cleaning*
Light	Silks, voiles, lawns	Programme 4	√
Soft	Polyester/cotton, light wool, medium polyesters	Programme 4	√
Medium	Heavy cotton, wool, linen, medium dress weight fabrics	Programme 4	√
Heavy	Satin, brocade, heavy cotton, bridal wear	Programme 4	√

IRON-ON VILENE

Weight	*Suitable for :*	*Washing*	*Dry cleaning*
Transparent	Lawn, voile, chiffon	Programme 8	√
Soft	Polyester cotton, lightweight dress fabrics	Programme 4	No.
Firm	Heavy cotton, linen, wool, medium dress fabrics	Programme 4	No.
Superdrape (stretch)	All knitted fabrics, wool, tweed	Programme 4	√

3.11 Fabrics

Many plain or small print fabrics are suitable. Avoid large prints unless you are ready to take the trouble, and the extra fabric, necessary for matching up the pattern at the centre seams. Avoid checks and stripes if you are not very experienced.

If you are top-heavy you could make the bodice in a dark colour and the skirt lighter or to lessen broad hips make the skirt dark and the top light. Do not do this if you are very short because it will make you look shorter.

Suggested fabrics
Crimplene or other polyester jersey
Courtelle jersey or other acrylic jersey
Brushed rayon   Viyella
Rayon and cotton mixtures
Polyester and cotton

Haberdashery
25cm (¼yd) or a pre-pack of light or medium weight Vilene
2 Reels Drima thread
55cm (22in.) Lightning nylon zip
Waist length + 7·5cm (3in.) curved petersham
5cm (2in.) Velcro
Few small pieces of Wundaweb

3.12 Yardage and layout

The amount of material you need depends on the width of the fabric and on the size of your pattern pieces. There are at least five different standard widths of fabric available, and, depending on what you choose, it may have to be cut one way because of the weave or the pattern, or you may

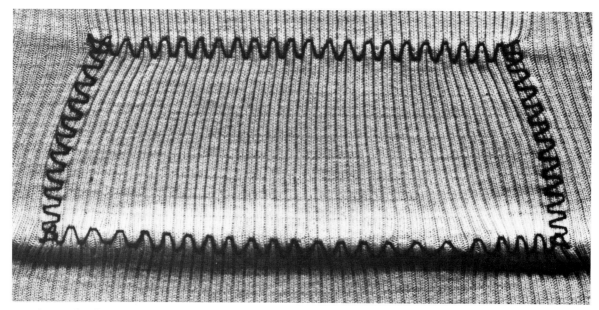

4   *A stretchy-knit fabric (courtesy Bernina Sewing Machines Ltd)*

have to match up checks and all this takes extra material.

There are many pattern sizes too, and after alterations to length and width have been made the quantity of material needed by each individual varies considerably.

After calculating what you used for the basic dress, make a note of it for future reference. When you begin on the adaptations in the book the amount will vary, but it could be useful later if you have a record of how many metres (yards) each one took.

The following is a way of calculating yardage and layout on plain fabrics or those not requiring any matching. Additional information on calculating for patterns and checks is given in those sections where these fabrics are suggested.

Preparation

Use an old sheet, a length of very cheap material, or Vilene to make a guide. Prepare several yards of this at least 165cm (64in.) wide. If using Vilene or narrow material, join it down the centre.

Using felt pens of different colours, mark off along one edge every 25cm ($\frac{1}{4}$yd), and draw in the widths of fabric across it, from 20cm (27in.) up

to 150cm (60in.) (Fig. 1). Some fabric is 115cm (66in.), so either join another piece on or remember there is extra width when laying the pattern out.

You then use this marked length for experimenting with the pattern pieces. Try it folded double, partly folded, opened out etc., to find the most economical way of cutting.

Layout

There is nothing mysterious about laying out a pattern for cutting out. There are three things to check with each pattern piece:

(i)   Is the straight grain line on the pattern on the straight of the fabric? – this should always be the lengthwise grain where possible.

70 cm (27 in)

90 cm (36 in)

115 cm (45 in)

140 cm (54 in)

150 cm (60 in)

(I)

(ii) Is the pattern marked FOLD anywhere? If so this must go to a folded piece of fabric, a small piece could be folded after the main sections have been cut.

(iii) Is it to be cut on double or single material?

This basic dress pattern is easy because there are no FOLDS to worry about. Lay out the bodice and skirt pieces all in one direction if fabric is knitted or one-way, or dovetailing them on plain fabric (Figs. 2a&b). Facings can always be cut from the scraps, but if you want to be quite certain you have enough then also position the facing pattern. As the pattern has been altered to fit, the pieces can be close together.

(2a) Fabric with nap, pile or one-way design

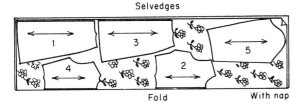

(2b) Without nap, pile or one-way design

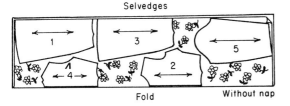

(both on lengthwise grain of fabric)

3.13 Cutting out

Work on a large flat smooth surface

For various reasons it is best to fold the fabric with the right side out when cutting out. It enables you to spot a flaw and avoid it in time; you can clearly see any regular pattern such as spots, stripes etc., and also even with an all-over design it helps to be able to place the pattern so that the print is balanced. When working with large prints or checks or any design to be care-

fully matched, it is essential to work on the right side, with the fabric single, not folded.

At one time it was thought safer to put the right side inside to protect it, and indeed if you are working on a pale plain expensive material such as might be used for a wedding dress, then you may feel happier to do so, but the right side will soon have to be exposed in order to sew the garment.

(i) Lay the fabric out right side out, folded with the selvedges together but not stretched. To ensure that it is flat take hold of the selvedge of the top layer and shake or flap the material, quickly bringing down the selvedge in the correct position.

(ii) If the fabric is inclined to slip, place a few pins down the selvedge. Don't use too many because there would be more likelihood of cutting across one with your scissors which will damage the blade.

(iii) Put the edges together at the cut end and hold with a few pins if necessary. Smooth the fabric across the fold and insert a few pins. If you can't get the whole length on the table, roll up part of it while you smooth out the remainder.

(iv) Place each pattern piece roughly in position and hold down with something, e.g. pin box, scissors, ruler. Lay out all the pieces in this way to check that it all goes on.

(v) Pin each piece in position first lining up the straight grain line with the fabric grain. Do this by measuring an even distance from the selvedge. Pin the straight grain with two pins. Pin the rest of each piece, using very few pins. Place them well inside the fitting lines to ensure that the edge of the pattern remains flat and insert all pins on the bias so that the fabric 'gives' under pinning and doesn't lift.

(vi) Take a last look to see that grains are correct, folds are to the folded edge of the fabric, etc., and then cut out.

The most accurate way to cut out is with the pattern to the right of the scissors (or to the left if you are left handed). In this way your eyes are directly above the edge of the pattern and therefore you can see the fabric clearly as you cut, which is what matters most. Also, this position means that you are not leaning across your body or putting too much weight on the scissors.

Cut with long strokes using three-quarters of the blade length. Cut right to the tip of the scissors each time. If you are left with a short piece to cut, open the scissors just sufficiently to make the cut. This is a skill which is quite quickly acquired once you know what it is you are working out.

As you move the scissors forward make sure you insert the apex of the open blade exactly in the cut of the fabric, to avoid a stepped edge.

At curves, open the blade wide and carve round the curve gradually closing the scissors. Never snip round a curve. If the curve is in an awkward position, cut all other edges, then cut straight across the curve, lift that piece away from the rest and finish cutting out.

As you cut out use your other hand to lift the fabric away. You achieve a much cleaner cut if the piece actually lifted by the lower blade is held at that height, say 6mm–1·3cm ($\frac{1}{4}$–$\frac{1}{2}$in.) while cutting. This hand is positioned slightly behind the scissors, peeling away the spare fabric completely. (Fig. 1.)

When you reach a corner, cut 6mm ($\frac{1}{4}$in.) or so past it (Fig. 2), lift the spare fabric right over to the side, move round and continue cutting.

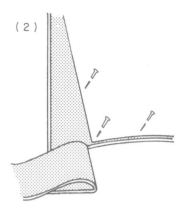

(2)

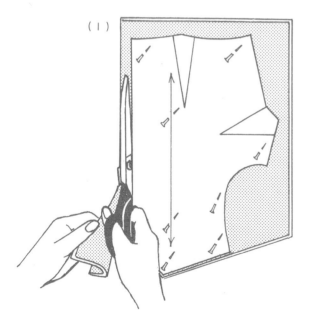

(1)

It is essential to move round and round the table when cutting out. Small pieces can be moved, but do not move the whole length while it has the pattern pinned to it.

If your fabric is suitable, and if you have to remove the pattern immediately after cutting, as you would when mounting for instance, you may like to chalk round each piece instead of pinning and take the pattern off altogether for cutting out.

Provided you use sharp chalk, long firm sweeping strokes with the edge of the chalk, not the corner, and use a ruler for straight lines, this is a better way of cutting out because the pattern is not in the way, you can work faster and it is generally much more enjoyable.

To use cutting out scissors properly, rest the flat underside on the table and lift only the handle slightly to cut. The blade remains on the table and slides along. People who try big scissors by lifting them completely and waving them in the air, lifting the points up high, will always think the scissors are heavy. In fact they are carefully balanced for use in that one position and you feel no weight at all. This is one reason why they should be kept for cutting out and not used for trimming or other jobs performed when the actual fabric is held in the hand.

If you cannot lay out the whole length of fabric, prepare it a section at a time, putting a few pins in the selvedges. Roll it up as you do this and then place the pattern pieces in position, lightly chalking round them instead of pinning. Re-roll the fabric up as you go along (Fig. 3) and if, when

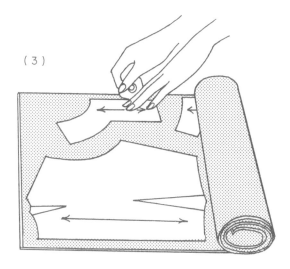

(3)

you come to the end, all pieces have gone on satisfactorily, pin and cut out one pattern piece at a time.

3.14 Marking turnings and darts

There is a certain amount of information on the pattern which must be transferred to the material before removing the pattern.

The conventional method which is used by tailors is the most satisfactory because it is quick, it can be used on every fabric, it marks both sides of the material, it stays put for as long as you want it to, and it is easily removed afterwards without marking the fabric. However, I think there is a case for sometimes using two other methods with certain fabrics and certain garments, so I am including marking with dressmakers' carbon paper and machine tailor tacking in this section. Whichever method you choose, start by marking any pieces cut to a fold in the fabric. Using tacking

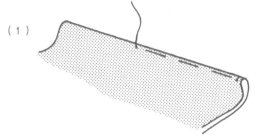

(1)

thread, run a row of tacking along the fold lifting the edge so that you can work along the top of the fold and there is no risk of catching the two layers in the needle. (Fig. 1.)

Tailor tacking

To all unbelievers who grumble that tailor tacking takes too long, I have always changed their attitude by persuading them to try this method which is the one tailors have always used, and to stand up to do it, since that makes you work faster.

(i) Prepare the pattern. Having already placed pins in position correctly for cutting out, they are not in the way now you come to tailor tack so fold back the pattern on the fitting line and crease firmly (Fig. 2). Snip any curves so that it will lie

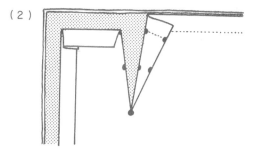

(2)

flat. If your pattern is made of Vilene, you may have to anchor the corners with a pin. To fold back darts, cut the pattern along one side of the dart. Alternatively, if you have tried out your basic pattern already and have no more extensive alterations to make, it is more satisfactory to cut off the turnings altogether, then you can tailor tack much more easily. If you do this remember to write in large letters on each piece that turnings must be allowed every time the pattern is used.

(ii) Thread your needle, No. 5 or 6 between, with a long piece of tacking thread and pull it through double but do not make a knot. Never use sewing thread for this because the tufts will slip out as you handle the garment. Tacking thread is soft and furry and the pieces will remain in the fabric. Also, it is very unsatisfactory to use single thread, the two pieces anchored in the same place will stay firmly in place.

(iii)   Place work with raw edges towards you and stitch as close as possible to the edge of the pattern (Fig. 3). Take up the smallest amount

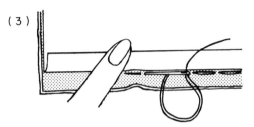

(3)

of fabric that you can, on the needle, helping it on with the forefinger of your left hand and without lifting the edge of the fabric. Leave stitches on the surface about 2·5cm (1in.) long although on long straight seams they can be longer. At the end of the thread simply cut and leave the ends.

(iv)   On sections where you might need closer marks to guide you, take smaller stitches but leave a small loop of thread on the surface. (Fig. 4.)

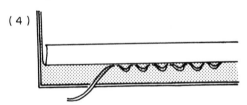

(4)

(v)   With darts, you will find it helpful to make one tack right at the point.

(vi)   Work all round each piece in this way and then, if there are other marks within the pattern that you need, such as centre front line if there is an overlap, fold the pattern back again to this new line and mark it. (Fig. 5.)

(vii)   Balance marks and other indications such as the depth of the neck slit, position of sleeve opening, sleeve head, zip, etc., make one tailor

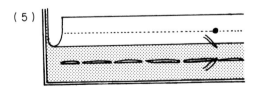

(5)

tack at right angles to the seam line.

(viii)   Remove the pattern pieces. Snip all the loops of thread. (Fig. 6a.)

(ix)   Sit down so that your eye level is lower and carefully part the layers of fabric, snipping each

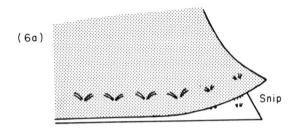

(6a)

Snip

thread as soon as you can see enough of it to do so. (Fig. 6a.)

Separate the layers and you can see that the exact shape of the pattern marked on both pieces and on both sides. However carefully you did the cutting out you can also see that it is vital to transfer these markings for the sake of accuracy. If tailor tacking a long straight edge and marks are not needed very close together, make short tufts as follows:

Take the first stitch and then two or three more, some distance apart. Pass needle to other hand and pick up medium-sized scissors, pull thread slightly taut and cut thread at first stitch on surface, close to where it emerges. Pull thread right through to leave a short end starting the next stitch; cut thread, pull through, cut thread and so on. Work only three or four stitches at a time. (Fig. 6b.)

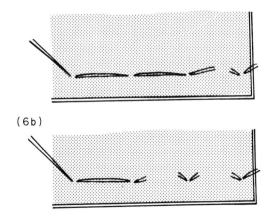

(6b)

The tiny tufts of thread will not fall out; if yours do then one of the following things is wrong:

(i) Stitches on surface too long, therefore long threads left trailing after snipping, fingers, scissors, etc., catch them and pull them out.

(ii) Not using correct tacking thread, sewing threads are smooth and shiny and will slip out.

(iii) Taking too much fabric up on needle so making a wide 'U' stitch which is loose instead of a tight 'V'.

(iv) Using too big a needle. Needle makes a big hole which thread does not fill and so it falls out.

Dressmakers' Carbon Paper

I don't find this method any quicker than tailor tacking, nor is it more accurate. In fact on some fabrics you have to press very hard and this tends to push the top layer of material to a different position. However, on mounted garments made from opaque fabrics, not the sheer ones, you can mark the mounting only with carbon paper.

You will need a metal toothed tracing wheel (Fig. 7) and a fairly large piece of hardboard to protect your table. The packets of paper now only contain blue, orange and white – other colours such as red often bled and spread to the top

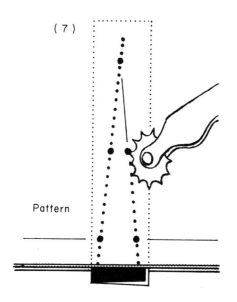

(7)

Pattern

fabric. Use white paper on dark fabrics and on white, use blue and orange on mixtures with white in them. If you are marking only the mounting fabric, as I suggest, use orange paper so that it is easily visible. White marks will show as dull marks on white fabrics but they are difficult to find and you will defeat the object by slowing down the construction while you search for the markings.

If you mark outer fabric with carbon paper you must only mark the wrong side; if you are marking mounting then you need the lines on the right side of the material. Whereas with top fabric you cut with the right side outside, with the few exceptions mentioned later such as velvet, for mounting that you intend to mark with carbon paper, fold the fabric for cutting out with the right side inside and then it is ready for marking.

(i) Cut the carbon paper into strips about 5cm (2in.) wide, or, with small sheets, cut into two. Fold strips in half with coloured carbon outside.

(ii) Place fabric on board and make sure it is lying smoothly. Slide carbon paper between the two layers of fabric. If you have to remove any pins make sure that the fabric remains flat as you slide in the paper.

(iii) Run tracing wheel, pressing firmly, along all pattern lines, allowing lines to cross at corners and dart points for accuracy. Remove carbon paper and pattern.

If for any reason you do cut out with the wrong side out, then use two pieces of paper and slide one face down on top of the upper layer of fabric and the other underneath face up.

After mounting the fabric onto this marked backing a few lines will have to be transferred as you will later need to see them from the right side. These include hems and necklines. Do this by running a row of tacking along the carbon line, taking the stitches through to the top fabric.

Tailor tacking by machine

This is useful if you have a lot of marking to do quickly or for marking out basic patterns on sheeting or Vilene.

Put tacking thread on the top of the machine

with normal thread below. Set the machine to a small zig-zag and the longest stitch. Raise the needle to its highest point and attach the special tailor tacking foot. Loosen the top tension, or you can remove the top thread completely from its tension control. Pass thread to the rear of the foot. Machine round all pieces beside the folded pattern edge. Remove work and snip the tacks between the two layers of fabric.

These instructions apply to the Bernina 830, for other machines check first with your instruction book.

3.15 Tacking

People in a desperate hurry sometimes only pin their seams before machining but the top layer of material always moves under the pushing pressure of the machine foot and it takes very little longer to tack properly. Also, everything has to be fitted first and it is a simple matter to pull out a row of tacking.

Tacking by hand
Use a larger needle than for permanent hand sewing; No. 5 for heavy fabrics and No. 6 for fine ones. Thread with tacking thread, putting a knot in the end. Tack all long seams with the work flat on the table; only shaped pieces should be lifted for tacking. Place one piece of fabric right side up with the raw edge towards you and the other, on top right side down. Ease the top piece into position by lifting and jerking rather than by pulling. It may be necessary with clinging fabrics to lift and flap the whole piece several times settling the raw edge down in position first and allowing the remainder of the piece to fall where it will. There must be no pulling or wrinkling or distortion of grain at these edges.

Match up the seam lines carefully and begin to tack. There should be no need to pin except where patterns are to be matched (see later sections).

Pick up a small amount, about 6mm ($\frac{1}{4}$in.), on the needle, easing the fabric onto the needle with the forefinger of your other hand (Fig. 1a). The size of the stitch left on the surface should vary

(1a)

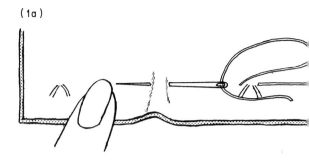

according to the position on the garment and if it is to be fitted, the strain likely on that part.

For example, if tacking up long seams on a full skirt the stitches can be 5cm (2in.) long, shoulder and bodice seams – no bigger than 1·3cm ($\frac{1}{2}$in.) and the same on sleeves and on trousers. You can work uneven tacking, which is a compromise between small and large stitches, taking alternately one large and one small (Fig. 1b). Whatever

(1b)

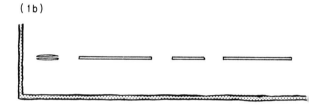

the size of the surface stitch never pick up more than 6mm ($\frac{1}{4}$in.) on your needle as this is what holds the two layers together.

Fasten off your thread with two backstitches but do not pull the thread tight at this point.

Jersey or Stretch fabrics
To ensure that you retain the 'give' in the seam, work about 15cm (6in.) of tacking then stretch that section of material allowing more thread to be taken up, tack another 15cm (6in.) pull, and so on.

Darts
To tack darts lift the material and fold it so that you can line up the stitching lines. Place a couple of pins across the dart to hold, one about half-way down and the other just below the point. Where possible tack from the raw edge towards

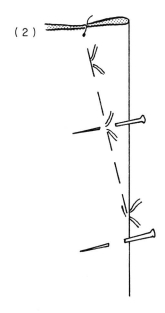

(2)

there is ease to be inserted, tack by hand. Machine tacking is also very useful where you simply want to see the effect of an idea before you begin to construct it, and also for making up basic patterns in calico, sheeting or Vilene ready for fitting.

Removal of tacking

Snip the backstitch at the end, take hold of the knot at the other end and pull. The thread should come out easily. If it is held by machine stitches anywhere the tacking thread will simply break and will not harm the fabric or the machining. If stitches need removing individually, use a bone or plastic bodkin specially made for this purpose, never the points of scissors.

Tacking threads that pull out in one unbroken length can be re-used.

3.16 Mounting

If a garment has been mounted it means that after cutting out, each piece of fabric has been tacked onto another backing material and the two layers then handled as one. Other terms used to describe this process are backing or underlining. A lining, on the other hand, is a separate shape made from the same or similar pattern pieces, hung inside the garment when nearly finished and attached at various points. The reason for lining is to allow it to slip easily over other clothes and is therefore used in coats and jackets. With most other garments it is better to mount although if a loosely woven soft fabric is used for a coat it can be mounted first for support and then lined for comfort.

Reasons for mounting

Providing support for the top fabric will considerably reduce creasing in wear, and in the case of fitted skirts and dresses it will also prevent seating. The heavier the person the more strain she places on her fabric in wear, so mounting is a great advantage. The very slim person who always buys top quality very expensive material does not have to mount for reasons of strain or

the point, fasten off with one back stitch (Fig. 2). This is because the end of your machining will come just at the dart point and it is difficult to remove a knot or an accumulation of thread from beneath the machining right on the fold.

If the dart comes on the bias of the fabric treat it in the same way as for jersey fabrics and pull it before fastening off the thread.

Direction of tacking

Try to tack in the direction that you will eventually be machining. This ensures that there is no slight shifting of seams.

Tacking by machine

Many makes of machine, e.g. Bernina, can quickly be adjusted to tack or baste. A needle with a higher eye than normal is used, adjust the stitch length to medium or large, depending on the fabric. Use sewing thread. Pin the seam first, placing pins across the seam, stitching right up to them before removing.

Use machine tacking for long seams, particularly where you have several to sew, but in shaped areas such as armholes, or curved seams, or where fabric support, but she may nevertheless like to do it because the whole silhouette is crisper and more shapely and the outfit remains looking fresh and new for much longer. Mounted fabric is much easier to sew, slippage of seams is less likely, puckering is eliminated, pressing is easier because seam imprints are less likely. Also hems never show because the stitching is taken only through the mounting.

Mounted garments travel better because they crease less, both in the suitcase and being worn.

Fabrics that need to be mounted

While all material can be made up alone, the following will give a better performance if mounted:
(a)   Loosely woven wools, soft mohair or angora
(b)   Soft rayons that may crease
(c)   Soft, thin cottons
(d)   Linen, 'linen-look' fabrics such as Moygashel
(c)   Brocade or silk that may crease or tend to hang in folds close to the body
(f)   Sheer fabrics that need to be made opaque, so that seams etc. do not show
(g)   Synthetic jersey such as Crimplene or nylon or Tricel jersey, not to prevent creasing but to lessen the possibility of creeping and clinging due to static electricity
(h)   Any inexpensive fabric can be improved beyond belief by mounting because it will then behave as a better fabric not as a cheap one.

Garments which need mounting

There are two things to consider. First, if you are using a fabric which will not perform as you want it to as a single layer, then you must mount it, whatever the garment. Examples under this heading would include chiffon, linen, and very soft open Bernat Klein type tweeds.

Secondly, if you are making a garment which by its style puts a strain on the fabric, you should mount it. Examples of this include all close fitting articles such as dresses and skirts.

You must decide, with each garment you make, according to the fabric, whether or not to mount it, but a few examples of which to mount and which

sections to mount are these:
(a)   Tweed suit. Either mount the whole and also loose line, or mount the skirt only and loose line the jacket
(b)   Crimplene dress. If you suffer from static problems, mount the whole thing
(c)   Woollen dress. Mount to prevent creasing but if too heavy, loose line or wear a slip
(d)   Nylon Blouse. Blouses are not usually mounted as they are loose fitting, but the front and back bodice can be mounted if not required see-through
(e)   Chiffon evening dress. Mount bodice for support, loose line full skirt to keep billowy
(f)   Cotton dress. Mount bodice and skirt for support, but not sleeves
(g)   Jersey Jump Suit. Mount if flimsy light fabric, but if in Courtelle jersey, Crimplene, etc., do not mount or line
(h)   Crimplene or other synthetic jersey Tunic and Trousers. Mount tunic to reduce static and allow to slip over other clothes but trousers would be too bulky if mounted
(i)   Trousers. These are not usually mounted although if using a lightweight fabric it certainly improves them. You would have to mount sheer cottons, voiles, chiffon, etc. and you can also mount trousers in brushed rayon, Viyella, crêpe etc., but anything heavy would probably become too bulky
(j)   Skirts. All straight or A line skirts should be mounted and also pleated skirts if made from cotton, rayon or creasing fabrics.

There are some fabrics which can never be mounted such as seersucker and pleated materials.

Fabrics for mounting

The success of mounting depends on the correct choice of the supporting fabric and this may be a further deciding factor. If you are unable to buy a suitable mounting, or you are not sure what to use, then it is better not to do it.

Occasionally people complain that mounted clothes are hot, which surprises me until I see the variety of underwear they are still wearing. Mounting can replace a slip and I find summer clothes much cooler because they stand away from the body. I think it is an excuse though because after people have become converted to mounting they find themselves automatically considering the mounting angle when they buy the fabric, and so choosing the weight accordingly. The other excuse is that it takes longer to make the garment and on the occasions I have set students to work in order to refute this they have been amazed that it has taken only an extra hour or so to do.

It is, of course, more expensive to mount, although you eliminate the cost of lining in most cases, but if you finish up with a longer lasting outfit then it is surely worth it.

Suggestions for mounting the main fabrics are:
(a)   Use cotton lawn, Vincel/cotton or any soft, thin, cotton for mounting wool, tweed, linen, Viyella, brushed rayon, cotton and velveteen, and also firm pure silk is better on these than on silk.
(b)   Use light Terylene crêpe or other flimsy plain weave fabric, for mounting sheer or semi-sheer fabrics such as Tricelon, Voile, blouse crêpe.
(c)   Use self-fabric to mount chiffon, ninon etc., or a plain version of it if mounting a print or a pattern of any sort.
(d)   Use nylon jersey for mounting all knitted fabrics such as Crimplene, Acrylic jersey, Courtelle, nylon jersey, Tricel jersey.
(e)   Use acetate rayon jersey which has more stretch, for mounting stretch fabrics, stretch towelling, cotton jersey and acetate jersey.
(f)   Only use conventional lining fabric if you want a slippery effect under a pinafore dress, dress or skirt made from a woollen suiting, flannel, Terylene or Trevira suiting etc., if you prefer it to a loose lining; only use good rayon lining from John Lewis & Co or Irwin Davis Ltd.

Buy the fabric first

Buy your fabric and have it with you when you buy the mounting, placing it on top of various mountings to feel the effect. The top material should be supported, but it should not have its character eliminated by a strong or opposite mounting. It should be lighter in weight unless you deliberately want some other effect, e.g., I have put cream satin under a black and silver striped organza.

Buy the same amount of mounting material unless you are omitting some part such as sleeves, in which case buy 50cm ($\frac{1}{2}$ yd) less for short or $\frac{3}{4}$ sleeves and 70cm ($\frac{3}{4}$ yd) less for long sleeves.

If you locate a supply of the most used mounting fabrics it is useful to buy a large amount for future use.

Colour

If the fabric is sheer or open, then a suitable colour of mounting must be found, but with solid fabrics white can be used for most things which is more economical than buying short lengths.

Shrinkage

Most reasonably priced material is now pre-shrunk as part of the finishing, but if you are doubtful and the fibre is rayon or cotton, wash and iron the whole length before cutting out.

Static electricity

It helps to eliminate static electricity if the length of nylon jersey and also the length of synthetic top fabric is washed through in a fabric softener such as Comfort before cutting out.

After making up, continue to rinse synthetic garments in one of these softeners.

How to mount

Mounting the garment is the first process.
(i)   Cut out your top fabric and then, without removing the pattern lift each piece onto your mounting material. Place with grain lines correct and lay them out as you did for the top fabric. The weight of the piece with the pattern pinned will hold it down without pinning further so cut round each piece.
(ii)   It is not usually necessary to mount facings, collars, cuffs or other pieces so at this stage only cut mounting for the main sections of the garment. If, later on, you decide to mount other parts, possibly because a print or turnings, show

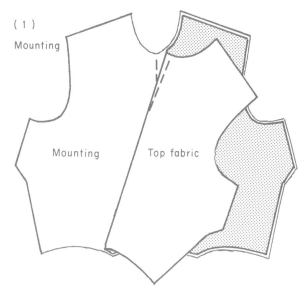

(1)

Mounting

Mounting   Top fabric

(vi)   Start at the centre of the piece, at the edge nearest to you and work a row of basting stitches up the middle to the far edge (Fig. 2). Take the needle across the body picking up 1·3cm ($\frac{1}{2}$in.) or so of fabric, pull it out at the left, move up and slightly right to re-insert it about 5cm (2in.) above the first stitch. Use the forefinger of the other hand to push the fabric onto the needle as it emerges to avoid having to lift the work off the table.

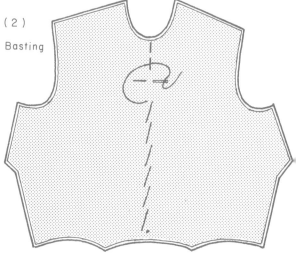

(2)

Basting

through, or because you find it behaves very differently when mounted, then these can easily be cut from the spare pieces.

(iii)   Look through the cut pieces and mark any folds, e.g., centre front line where fabric has been cut to a fold. Do this on the top fabric for the entire length of the pattern piece and on the mounting just for an inch or two at the top.

(iv)   Working on one piece at a time to avoid confusion, remove the pattern from the main fabric. Open out the corresponding pieces of mounting, wrong side up. Place the top fabric wrong side down, lining up straight edges and matching the tack along the centre if there is one. (Fig. 1.) There should be no need to pin, and indeed it is inadvisable to lift the fabric with pins, except in a few cases where pile or slippery fabrics are used in which case lightly put in two or three pins.

(v)   Thread your needle with a long piece of tacking thread. Use a normal size Between needle of suitable thickness for tacking on that particular fabric – the finer the material the finer should be the needle. Use tacking thread because it is soft and will not mark the work when pulled out. If working on velvet or silk chiffon or satin, you should use a finer thread such as Clarks Anchor Machine Embroidery No. 50, but never use permanent sewing thread for doing mounting.

(vii)   Do not pull the thread tight. If, at the end of a row you can see the fabric is puckered, snip the basting at that point to release it.

(viii)   Start another row by simply moving across and working down in the opposite direction. At the end of your thread, pull your needle out, leaving an end of thread. Fastening off tends to pucker it. (Fig. 3.)

(ix)   After working from the centre out to one side, return to the middle and cover the rest of the piece.

(x)   Work to within 1·3cm ($\frac{1}{2}$in.) or so of all raw edges and where you finish the thread at these outside edges work a single back stitch to fasten off. This will prevent the layers parting in handling.

(xi)   Baste all sections in this way. The basting must remain in position until the garment is quite finished.

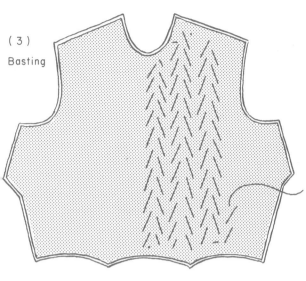

(3)
Basting

Marking turnings
Replace the pattern and pin in position. Mark all darts and turnings, with tailor tacking or with carbon paper.

Making Up
You now completely ignore the fact that you are working with two layers and proceed to make up the garment. The processes that apply to single fabrics are all used. For instance if darts are bulky they should be split open and pressed.

Turnings at necklines etc. are always layered and the mounting is treated as one more layer. Seam turnings within hemlines must be cut away and this is done whether or not the garment is mounted. Hems are easier to handle because you can press a softer fold line and stitches are not liable to show. Seams can be pressed without worry as there is a further layer of fabric to prevent marks showing through. Raw edges are neatened according to the top fabric, usually either with overcasting or zig-zag stitch. If the top fabric is particularly soft or is liable to fray badly you will find the mounting tends to hold it firm and so the neatening is easier to do.

Removing basting
Before the final press take hold of each knot and gently pull. Most threads will pull out easily but if you feel any resistance, snip and pull again.

If working on satin, velvet, or any shiny fabric it would be advisable not to do any firm pressing over the body of the garment until the basting has been removed. In fact, if the garment is in several sections, remove basting as soon as one part is complete. For example, remove basting between neck and waist join as soon as neck is finished and sleeves are in; on a long skirt, when only the hem remains to be done, remove all basting except for about a depth of 30cm (12in.) at the bottom.

3.17 Order of making up

(i)   Darts
(ii) Centre front seam, centre back seam
(iii) Side seams, bodice and skirt
(iv) Waist seam, shoulder seams
(v)   Neckline and zip
(vi) Sleeve
(vii) Hem length

The dress must be fitted and any alterations checked, between each of the above stages.

Tacking up for fitting
(i)   Tack bodice darts, CB seam, side and shoulder seams. Fit.
(ii) Tack skirt darts and seams. Fit.
(iii) Tack bodice to skirt. Fit.

3.18 Neck facing and interfacing

Neck facing

Front
(i)   Pin neckline of basic pattern on to paper.
(ii) Outline neck and shoulder, continue down centre front for 22cm (8½in.). This allows for depth of opening + 5cm (2in.); actual depth is adjusted at fitting. (Fig. 1.)
(iii) Remove pattern pieces. Mark in 1·5cm (⅝in.) turning inside line, round neck, front and shoulder. (Fig. 2.)
(iv) Using ruler or marker draw in facing

Neck facing for basic dressing

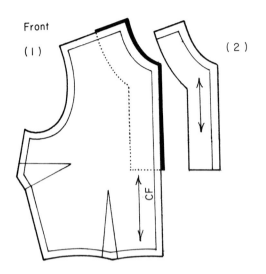

5cm (2in.) wide, measuring from fitting line. This allows 6mm ($\frac{1}{4}$in.) at outer edge for neatening. Cut out. Mark straight grain.

Back
(i) Fold and pin out neck dart on back bodice pattern.
(ii) Place on paper and pin down, keeping it flat round neck. Outline neck, shoulder and down centre back. (Fig. 3.)

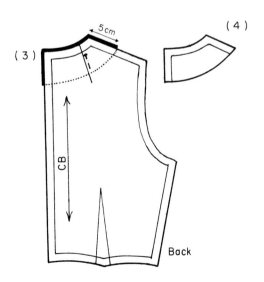

(iii) Remove pattern. Mark turnings and measure facing 5cm (2in.) wide all round. Mark in straight grain. Cut out. (Fig. 4.)
(iv) Pin down on to double fabric matching straight grain, cut out.

Interfacing neck

Attach after marking turnings etc. on garment. Use facing pattern or garment as a guide for cutting the interfacing. Fold interfacing in half and cut pieces for the back neck and for the front neck and front opening, making them slightly narrower than the facing width. (Fig. 5.)

Place each piece, granule side down, onto the wrong side of the garment. Do this at your ironing board, supporting the rest of the fabric to prevent stretching the neck. Arrange in position

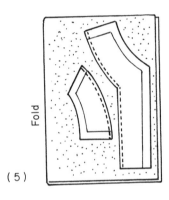

Interfacing basic dress

and press with steam iron or if using dry iron, anchor the pieces by pressing, then stick them more firmly by pressing again with a damp muslin and the iron a little hotter. Whichever method you like, press only from the raw edges inwards for about an inch or so, do not press over the raw edge of the Vilene at this stage, the remainder will gradually become stuck down as the work and pressing proceed.

3.19 Fitting

If you have to fit yourself you will find it easier if you tack the back seam right up and leave the

centre front seam open. You can then pin this up yourself quite accurately. Fold under one edge on the fitting line, lap it over the other edge and pin. Place pins horizontally, otherwise the front will tend to lift and become shorter. (Fig. 1.)

(1)

Pinning CF

Stand perfectly still and begin by noting any obvious areas of tightness or looseness. Turn sideways and look in the mirror, still standing still and turning only your head. To see the back view try propping another mirror up on a chair although if you sew a great deal it would be worth having a pair of mirrors arranged permanently.

You might also find it easier, if you are on your own, to try the garment on inside out the first time so that you can pin out excess fabric, or undo tacking in tight seams and so ensure that the adjustment is accurate. Do try it on the right way before you machine though, in case you have one side different from the other.

Whereas someone fitting you can undo a seam and re-pin it quite accurately on you, it is often better, when fitting yourself, to put in only one pin as a guide, making a mental note of the exact alteration needed as far as you can judge, for example, 6mm ($\frac{1}{4}$in.) all down a seam, or maybe nothing out at the armhole but sloping in 1·3cm ($\frac{1}{2}$in.) at the waist. Take the garment off, quickly make the alteration, using pins only if you are doubtful about it, and slip it on to see if it is better. Working like this on each area, you can then finally take it off and re-tack all alterations before slipping it on prior to machining.

What to wear

Even if you haven't just been to the hairdresser, wear an overall or button-through dress. It is the likelihood of messing up hair and make-up which leads people to reduce the number of fittings, not so much the effort of undressing. On warm summer days I wear a bikini to sew in and the garments go on top for fitting. But, always wear the right shoes as they affect posture. Incidentally, you will discover a lot more about fitting and about the way fabrics behave if you prepare several items at once and fit them all.

There is no specific number of fittings necessary for a garment. Each must be tried on often enough to achieve a satisfactory fit. By making up a basic pattern initially you will be reducing considerably the number of fittings required by subsequent articles made from the same pattern.

Darts

(i) Bust darts

The shape produced by the dart should be sufficient for the bust, also allowing for arm movement. The dart should end about 1·3cm ($\frac{1}{2}$in.) away from the actual bust point, or movement will be restricted (Fig. 2a). On a tiny, slim figure the dart could be taken closer but on a larger person it may be more comfortable to shorten the dart.

If the bulge of fabric is insufficient for the bust the dart must be made a little wider at the base (Fig. 2b). lf there is too much shaping and the bust is not filling it, the dart should be made smaller at the base. (Fig. 2c.)

The point of the dart may be raised or lowered

so that it is on the same level as the bust point (Fig. 2d). To do this, undo the tacking almost to the base of the dart and re-pin, coming to a point at the correct position. If the dart point has to be moved more than about 1·3cm ($\frac{1}{2}$in.) then undo the whole dart and a section of the side seam and re-pin from a new base, higher or lower, whichever is required.

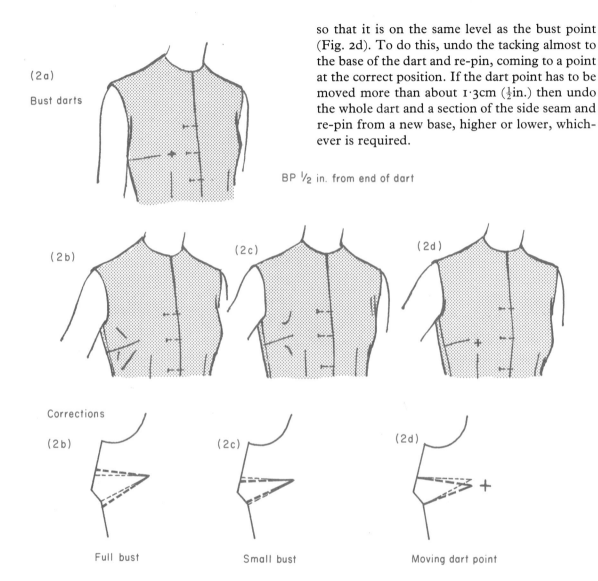

(2a)

Bust darts

BP $\frac{1}{2}$ in. from end of dart

(2b)

(2c)

(2d)

Corrections

(2b)

(2c)

(2d)

Full bust

Small bust

Moving dart point

_ _ _ _ _ _ _ Original fitting line

▬ ▬ ▬ ▬ ▬ New fitting line

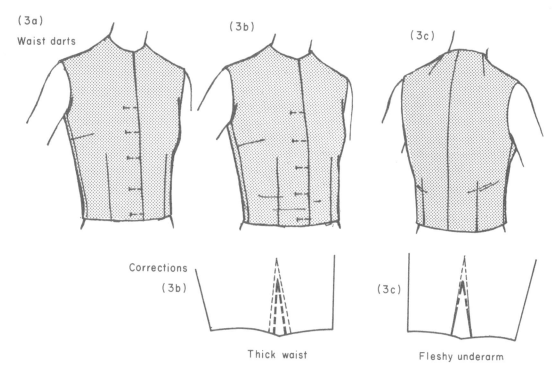

(3a)
Waist darts

(3b)

(3c)

Corrections

(3b)

(3c)

Thick waist

Fleshy underarm

(ii) Waist darts of bodice

Front darts should run up under the bust but not too close to it (Fig. 3a). On a short-waisted or low-busted figure they may look better fairly short. On a thick-waisted figure, reduce the width of the dart at the base (Fig. 3b). Waist darts should only be made wider at the base for the figure with a full bust and a small waist.

Back waist darts should run up to the widest part of the back. On a thick-waisted figure or one that is full under the arm and across the back these darts should be quite short.

(iii) Shoulder darts

The dart in the basic pattern has been placed close to the neck point in a position that is mid-way between a neck dart and the usual shoulder dart. This should produce the shaping needed by those who have rounded backs and those with protruding shoulder blades. However, as with all darts, there should be no surplus fabric or bulges left uncatered for, so examine the back carefully, looking for pockets of material. With a severely round back or back neck it may be better to

move the whole dart into the neckline. For a figure that is flat at the centre of the back but has wide-apart bony shoulder blades (often goes with square shoulders) move the dart along and into the shoulder seam. (Fig. 4.)

To move the dart, undo the tacking, smooth the fabric over that area and pick the surplus fold up in the position required, pinning to a point. It is important to move the arms when testing this particular area as these darts should also provide for ease of movement. A tightness can sometimes indicate that the darts are not in the best position for the figure.

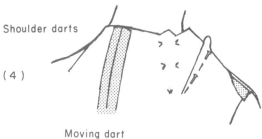

Shoulder darts

(4)

Moving dart

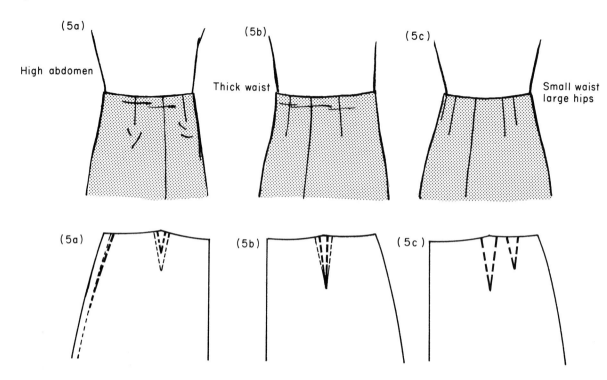

(iv) Front skirt darts

If the skirt seems tight over the stomach but there are pockets of fabric below, then shorten the darts to about an inch in length, at the same time making them smaller at the base (Fig. 5a). Do not increase the width of the dart at the waist in order to reduce the waist measurement, you should take in the side seams for this particular problem. (Fig. 5a.)

(v) Back skirt darts

These have to serve a dual function, that of reducing the waist and also providing enough shaping for the seat in movement. The thick-waisted figure is easier to fit as the darts can be reduced in width (Fig. 5b), but it is more difficult to fit the small waist–large hips figure. Increasing the width of the dart at the base usually results in an unattractive hour-glass effect so it is better to put in a second dart. (Fig. 5c.)

(vi) Elbow dart

This dart is used to insert shaping in a sleeve to allow for the arm bending. If it is too wide at the base the sleeve will appear to be drawn up, if too high or too low, the back of the dress will feel tight and uncomfortable. Check position by bending arm and see where the dart settles with the arm in this position.

The seams

(i) Centre back seam

Note any tightness or looseness, and release and re-pin. This seam on the basic dress is straight, but on some figures it can be shaped in at the waist and also a little at the neck (Fig. 1a). It can also be flared slightly at the hem (Fig. 1b). For a back that is narrow across the shoulder blades, take in the back seam all the way down to avoid altering the grain line and then let out the side seams to compensate. (Fig. 1c.)

(ii) Centre front seam

This seam can be adjusted for those figures with broad or narrow chests and also for hollow chests (Fig. 2a). Release tacking and repin, but,

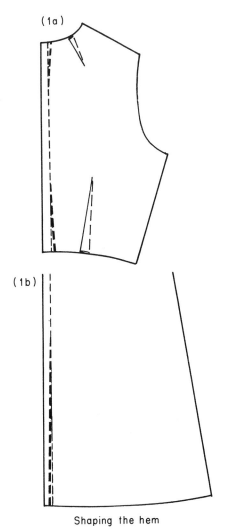

(1a)

(1b)

Shaping the hem

(1c)

Narrow back

Back

as with the centre back, if you are taking it in above the armhole, you will have to pin out an even amount right down the seam or the grain of the fabric will be distorted. It may also be necessary to undo the shoulders and move the whole bodice inwards towards the neck. Re-pin the shoulders. The surplus turnings at the neck and armhole should not be trimmed off until after the neckline and armhole have been established. (Fig. 2b.)

Front

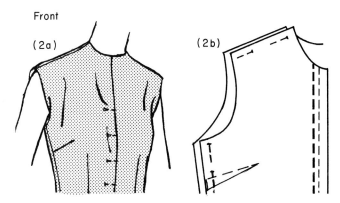

(2a)

(2b)

On the small waisted figure the seam can be taken in below the bust (Fig. 3a), but take care not to then let out the skirt seam to provide room for a stomach bulge as it will tend to emphasize it. Instead, let out darts and side seams for this problem.

The centre front seam may be flared slightly at the hem.

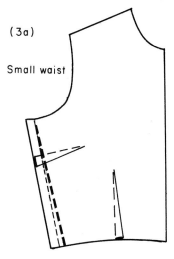

(3a)

Small waist

(iii) Side seams of the bodice

These should be fitted as closely as the wearer can tolerate. The exact amount of ease needed will depend on the fabric being used and also on the size of the person, but a bodice that is too loose will present problems with setting in the sleeve and in wear it will be uncomfortable.

For a thick waist let out the seams; for a small waist, take them in, sloping from the armhole. (Fig. 3b.)

(3b)

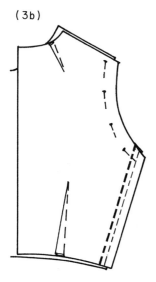

(4a)

Skirt
seams

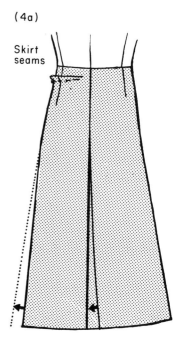

For a narrow back, release the seam and take in the back only, remarking the armhole line. A few women have a large rib cage or diaphram which necessitates letting out the front only and the centre front seam can also be used.

(iv) Skirt seams

Balance: These should hang at right angles to the floor. If the seam swings to the front, lift the skirt at the back waist, pinning out a fold until the seam is straight. (Fig. 4a.) If it swings towards the back, lift the front waist in the same way. (Fig. 4b.)

Width: Next see whether the width is correct. If there is surplus fabric pin it out either all the way down, or, on a straight or rectangular figure, only below the hips. (Fig. 4c.)

Thighs: If the thighs are heavy try letting out the centre front and centre back seams rather than the

(4b)

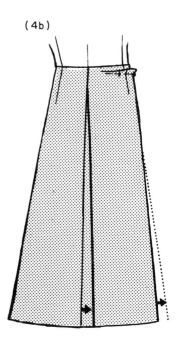

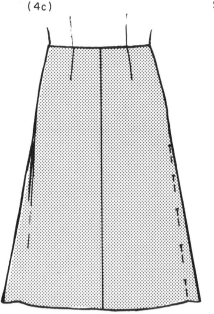

(4c)

Sleeve seam

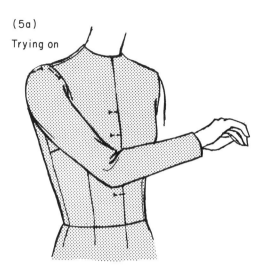

(5a)

Trying on

side seams; it will emphasize the bulge less.

Hip depth: If the skirt appears tight from the waist down to the hips, lift the whole skirt by pinning out a fold right round the waist. This may be in addition to the balance alteration. (Fig. 4d.)

Plump top arm: the pattern has been altered to allow for this but it may be necessary to let the seam out still further above the elbow. (Fig. 5b.) *Muscular lower arm*: straighten the seam slightly from elbow to wrist.

Small wrist: slope the seam in for the bottom 13cm (5in.) of the seam.

Finally, make sure the hand will slip through the wrist easily.

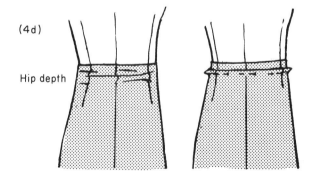

(4d)

Hip depth

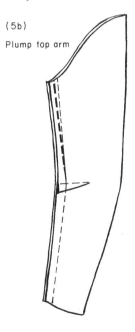

(5b)

Plump top arm

(v) Sleeve seam

Fit this seam by slipping the sleeve onto the arm, anchor with a few pins over the top and bend the arm. It should feel comfortable but there should be no surplus width. Fit it more tightly in a jersey fabric than a woven one. (Fig. 5a.)

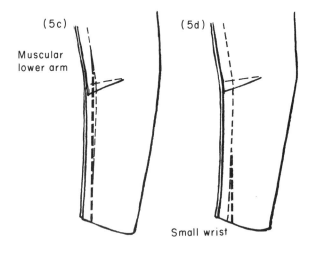

(5c)

Muscular
lower arm

(5d)

Small wrist

(vi) Waist and shoulder seams
Work on both at the same fitting as they affect
each other.
Hollow waist: look for folds of fabric across the
back. They may be on the bodice, or skirt, or
both. (Fig. 6a.) Pin out the surplus fabric,
running the alteration to nothing at the side
seams. (Fig. 6b.)

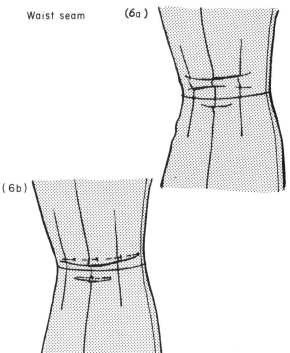

Waist seam   (6a)

(6b)

Short waist: if there is surplus fabric all round, or
possibly only at the front, above the waist, then
pin out the fold to raise the waistline. (Figs.
6c&d.)

The waist join should run round the figure at
the most comfortable point for the wearer, at
the same time remembering her figure faults. A
short-waisted person should try to wear her waistline a little below her natural waist, a long-waisted

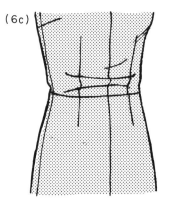

(6c)

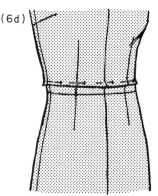

(6d)

figure looks better balanced if the waistline is
high. The person with short legs should try to
lengthen her skirt by having a high waistline. If
the natural waistline is uneven it is usually best
to try to disguise the fact. For example, a hollow
back waist usually means a dipping waistline and
if you fit the waist join exactly it will emphasize
the irregular waist. Make sure the garment is
comfortable by lowering it slightly, but disguise
the fault by not taking it too low.
Shoulders: the folds of fabric described in the first

Shoulder seams

(7a)

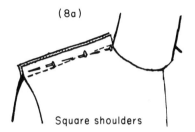

(7b)

Sloping
shoulders

out of the centre back seam. The front is usually unaffected because the shoulder bone protrudes and supports the fabric.

Square shoulders: release the shoulder seam at outer edge, leaving joined at neck edge and re-pin, raising the seam at the armhole edge and also taking a little off at the neck. (Fig. 8a.)

(8a)

Square shoulders

Hollow chest: even if the centre front seam has been taken in, it may be necessary to lift surplus fabric in this area into the shoulder seam. Lift the front only. (Fig. 8b.)

(8b)

Hollow chest

two points in this section are sometimes caused by sloping shoulders or by a figure shortness between neck and underarm. If the armhole and darts look as though they could be raised, try lifting the shoulder seam and see if it takes on a better appearance and feels more comfortable.

Lifting the back shoulder only, will remove folds at the back waist or underarm, lifting the front will remove front surplus, and also may remove any armhole gape.

The opposite also applies: if the waist join is uneven or too high, try adjusting the shoulder seams.

Sloping shoulders: the shoulder seam should be lifted, usually on both back and front at the arm-hole edge, but not at the neck. (Fig. 7b.) Having done this you may find it necessary to take a little

Long back: if the dress is lifting in the middle of the back, release the shoulder seams at the neck end and re-pin. (Fig. 8c.)

(8c)   Long back

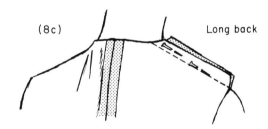

Neckline

The base of the neckline is difficult to establish and it is helpful to measure an existing dress, even if you know it is too high or too low, and start from there. Someone with a slim upright neck will probably want the neckline higher and tighter than someone with a broad based short neck; some people with a protruding top vertebra like a low neck at the back that won't cut across it. Very often too, it is not the centre front or centre back that is too low but simply that the neckline needs to be higher at the sides.

Examine the figure from the side, some necks slope forward and therefore the front neckline only needs lowering a little but the back remains the same or even needs raising a little (Fig. 9a). A very upright figure with shoulders held back can produce a neckline that is too wide at the back but pulling at the sides. In this case release the shoulder seams a little and take in the centre back seam. (Fig. 9b.)

Finally, on necklines, I am often told about dresses that 'ride up and choke me' and funny little drawings accompany the query. This is not a matter of altering the neckline itself but it is a question of balance, either the front is too long or the back is too short. Also, if the bust darts are too long or if the dress is tight across the chest this will make the riding up that much worse. The clearest way to see the problem is to put on a dress that does this, stand normally and ask someone to unpick a shoulder seam and lift the front up higher but let the back down, so creating a gap at the shoulder seam. Pin extra paper or fabric in here, take the dress off and it will be clear which section needs adding to, and which needs shortening in future, before cutting out. (Fig. 9c.)

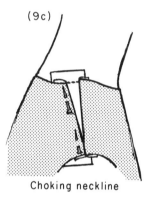

(9c)

Choking neckline

Length

Sleeve: this is very much a matter of choice but on the whole the person with short arms prefers a shorter sleeve, and the person with long arms likes the sleeve to come well down on to her wrist. Stand with arms hanging down to decide on the length.

Skirt: this depends on fashion to a certain extent and although it helps to make a note of a specific skirt length and work to it, the length will vary according to the style. For instance, a full short skirt in Terylene/cotton will have to be a little longer than a straight skirt in tweed.

The final edge must be an even distance from the floor regardless of a hollow waist, prominent bust or any other features.

Marking a hem with help: You can buy a hem-marker or you can attach a ruler to a firm block of wood with a couple of screws. (Fig. 10.)

Put on the right shoes and stand still on a smooth floor, not a thick pile carpet.

(9a)

Sloping neck

(9b)

Upright neck

(10)

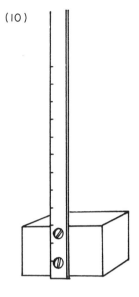

Hem marker

4

Basic trousers

With this pattern I have tried to overcome some of the problems that seem to occur with everyone. I have often found that darts, which are used partly to suppress the waist and partly to provide bottom shape, can look unattractive, particularly on the front, and produce too much shape. To remove the shape we take in the seams which then emphasize the hips and thighs.

The other fault that has occurred in just about everyone I have ever fitted is that of drooping and bagginess. Although the waist has always appeared to be in position I have often felt that I could take a horizontal seam right round the trousers to lift the excess folds. On this pattern, therefore I have eliminated the darts and put them into a curved seam thereby giving a smooth waistline and also providing a useful fitting point for lifting the trousers. This yoke seam is fairly high so that it will not emphasize the hips; in fact, on the contrary, it provides an interesting detail which draws the eye upwards. If you are slim and wear tucked-in blouses the seam looks attractive whereas if you don't usually emphasize your waist in trousers you will probably be wearing a top or jacket outside them anyway.

The front section of the crutch seam is straight, with only a slight curve (if this part is scooped out too much it causes horizontal creases), the back seam resembles a dog's hind leg, but this is the shape I have used on everyone for some time. This back seam should be very much on the cross to allow the fabric to stretch as you move each leg forward so I have shaped it in to the

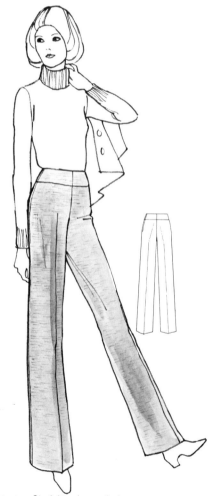

Trousers: Straight yoke, no darts
Straight leg
Side zip

waist to give an attractive and slimming effect, then out again to give hip width and finally scooped out under the crutch to eliminate those sagging folds, but up again at the fork to give a nice high fitting crutch. I have also extended the back fork a little to allow for those people who are thicker through from front to back, and also for heavy thighs. This can be taken in again if the leg is too wide at this point.

The leg is straight and fairly slim and can easily be shaped from the thigh line if more flare is needed. The leg length is long because nearly all trousers need lifting initially and so you will still have plenty to turn up.

4.1 Figure types

Not many women can boast that they are perfect trouser shapes and so we apply the same rules – those of disguise – as we do to other garments. Use plain dark matt cloth for the most slimming effect; wear a matching top to make you look taller (Fig. a), or a contrast to make you look shorter (Fig. b). If your hips are slim use a lighter colour but you can disguise a large bust with a dark top (Fig. c). Only wear tucked-in tops if you want to emphasize your waist (Fig. d). A short person will look shorter still in trousers with a long coat over, it would be better to draw attention to the shoulders to add height (Fig. e). If you wear a top over trousers to cover hip and thigh bulges, fit it slightly at bust and waist or even wear it belted to avoid a completely rectangular look (Fig. f). If your legs are short avoid long tops; instead wear tucked in shirts or waist jackets (Fig. g), or if you need to cover a bulge have the jacket just tipping the bulge and also looser at that point than the trousers.

4.2 Fabrics

I now confine myself almost entirely to jersey cloth for trouser outfits even if sometimes mixing it with a woven fabric for the top, because, on my figure, I simply cannot achieve a smooth close

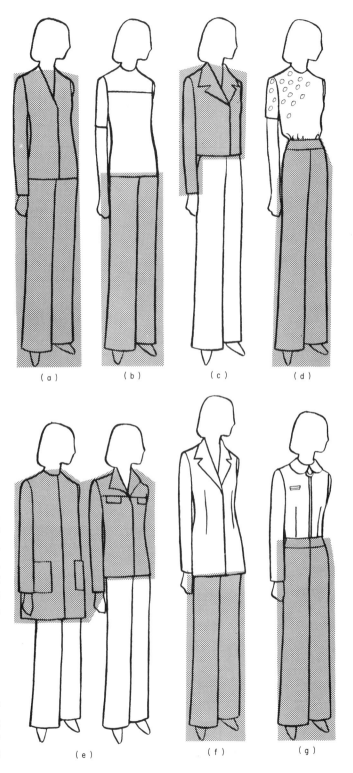

(a) (b) (c) (d)

(e) (f) (g)

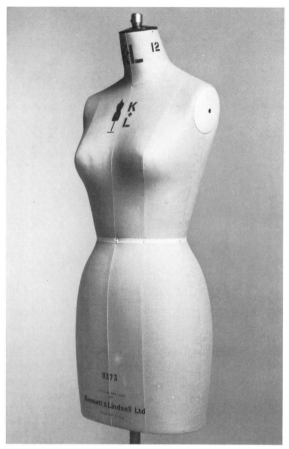

5   *The average woman (courtesy Kennett & Lindsell Ltd)*

fit round hips, thighs and waist, and yet still have ease, in a woven fabric. It seems that unless you have a slim bony figure with not much to move about when you walk, you are likely to find that the ease you must allow for movement, will show as looseness in a woven fabric. I only use a woven fabric for very wide legged evening trousers or culottes where the flare begins at the crutch on the inside leg and just above the hip on the outside leg. Then because of the width of leg and the style I choose a light weight fabric.

If you have trouser fitting problems you can at least make wearable trousers in jersey with room to move. If you think that this is going to be too restricting, have a look around and you may be surprised at the variety of fabrics that are jersey-backed. After all you can even buy jersey velvet.

The fabric suggestions are not, of course, restricted to jersey because there are many people for whom wovens present no problem.

Many people complain that they lose the creases in their trousers. There is no fabric that will withstand constant strain and movement without showing it and if you lose the creases only after considerable wear then you are lucky. If you have used a fabric that you have found difficulty in creasing anyway, then this would be one to avoid in the future. You must accept that, as with all garments, they crease and need re-pressing and they need washing or cleaning; if anything more often than other garments.

Trousers can be mounted to reduce the tendency to crease but it makes them rather bulky in the crutch area and they can also be too warm.

Fabric suggestions
It is advisable to use jersey fabric, especially for your first pair, as trousers in woven fabric are more difficult to fit. Choose a firm wool or synthetic knit with not too much give across the width.

Stitch with Drima which will 'give'; a medium length stitch, not too small, and a very slight zig-zag to prevent seams splitting. Neaten raw edges with a small zig-zag or just trim neatly.

Press with a medium-hot iron over damp muslin. Lift the muslin and the turnings will curl up so press again, then replace the damp muslin with a dry one and press again until the fabric is flat. If using a steam iron, open seams with it, then use the iron over the damp muslin, followed by the steam iron alone again. Leave the work to cool throughly before moving.

Creases in trousers should be put in by pressing over and over again with medium hot iron and damp muslin, finishing with dry cloth. The creases will not come out even in washing, although from time to time they will need re-pressing.

Fabric
1·5m (1½ yards) (or 1·25m (1¼ yards if short and

slim) or 1·4m (54in.) or 1·5m (60in.) fabric.

Haberdashery
1 reel Drima, Wundaweb for hems, 1 20cm (8in.) or 23cm (9in.) Lightning Concealed Zip, 7·5cm (3in.) Velcro.

4.3 Making the pattern

Make your trouser pattern on True Sew paper by following the diagram shown.

It is helpful to take a few measurements and compare them with the size of the pattern as there are some adjustments you can make before cutting out. You will find, though, with trousers, that some problems will not reveal themselves

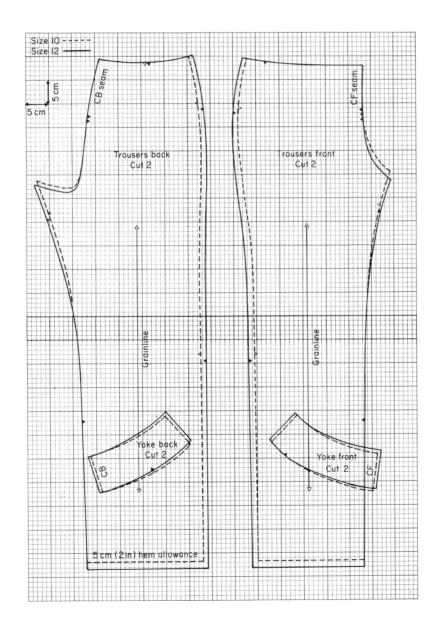

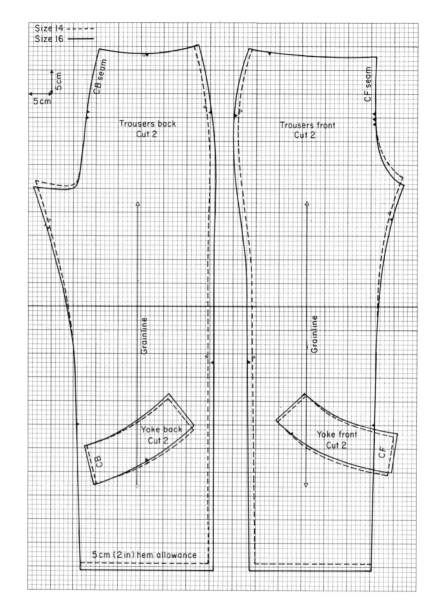

until you try them on, so it is probable that after your first pair, you will need to adjust the pattern still further before you are satisfied. In fact, if you have already encountered apparently insoluble trouser-fitting problems then regard your first pair using this pattern as totally experimental; not necessarily to be completed and worn unless for gardening (if enough room!). Use an odd length of fabric you've lost interest in; don't use sheeting or calico because there is insufficient weight in it to hang, which is what trousers are all about; and anyway, they will look so awful in sheeting that you won't want to go on with the fitting.

4.4 Checking the pattern

Pin yoke patterns to leg patterns, overlapping turnings.

(i) Inside leg

Take your inside leg measurement from crutch to ankle or, if you have a pair of trousers that are the right length, measure the seam (Fig. 1.1). Compare with the length of the inside leg seam on the pattern, allowing 5cm (2in.) for the hem, and then allowing a further 5cm (2in.) in case they have to be lifted at fitting. If pattern is very much too long then shorten by pleating at knee level.

(ii) Outside leg

Measure from waist to ankle and check the pattern (Fig. 1.2). If pattern is too short add extra evenly across the waist (it would normally be a very small amount), if pattern is too long, leave it as it is and take it off the waist or yoke seam at fitting.

(iii) Thighs

Measure both thighs (in case one is larger than the other) high up, almost at crutch level (Fig. 1.3). Measure across both pattern pieces, omitting turnings and allowing 4cm (1½in.) for ease. If too big, do not alter until fitting stage. If too small, add a little on the side seam in case you need it, but add an extra 2.5cm (1in.) at the fork on both back and front. To do this, extend the crutch seam following the curve of the seam, and run down into the inside leg seam about 13cm (5in.) below.

(iv) Crutch length

This is more difficult to check accurately because a lot depends on the shape of the figure and how much movement of bulk there is in walking, but at least it will give you an idea of what you may encounter when you come to fit.

Run the tape measure from front waist to back waist between your legs. Put the two pattern pieces together and measure the crutch seam. No ease needs to be allowed here as there will be a

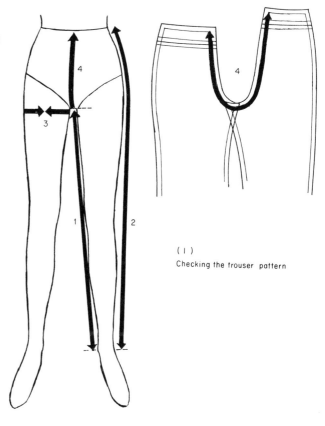

(I)
Checking the trouser pattern

lot of give in the seam (Fig. 1.4). If pattern seam is too long do nothing until fitting as you cannot tell whether you need to shorten it at the front waist, back waist (or both) or at crutch level. If it is too short, extend the fork on both back and front pattern as for big thighs. It may be that you have already added some on for thighs as these two things often go together, if so you shouldn't need to add much extra for crutch seam length.

These checks will not reveal all the faults, nor will they make the trousers fit, but at least you will know that you will be cutting them out wide enough and long enough, thus enabling you to fit them.

4.5 Cutting out

Place leg pattern pieces on folded fabric with grain correct, running down the leg. Never cut trousers across the width of the fabric. The two pattern pieces can be dovetailed if the material is two-way but one-way designs, prints, pile fabrics and all knitteds must be cut with the fabric running one way on all sections. Place the yoke sections in position matching the grain lines to the fabric grain (Fig. 1). Pin pattern in position

Trouser cutting out

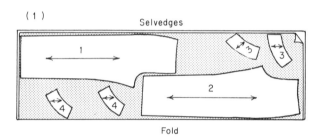

(1)

or anchor with a few small objects. Cut out and mark all turnings. Mark front crutch line from fork across to side seam. This should be tailor tacked as you need to see it from the right side.

If you feel you need to keep bulk to a minimum at the waist, or if you are using a heavy fabric, face the yoke with lining, cotton lawn, poplin or other light fabrics instead of cutting facings again from the top fabric.

4.6 Making up

Order of making up trousers

(i)   Tack yokes to legs
(ii)   Tack outside leg seams, leaving left side open for 23cm (9in.) at waist
(iii)   Tack inside leg seams. Press
(iv)   Fit one leg
(v)   Tack crutch seam
(vi)   Fit and adjust
(vii)   Take legs apart and machine and finish yokes inside and outside leg seams. Press

(viii)   Insert zip if putting in side seam
(ix)   Turn up and tack hems
(x)   Tack crutch seam. Fit
(xi)   Machine crutch seam. Insert zip if in centre front
(xii)   Attach facing to waist
(xiii)   Finish hems. Press

Tacking up for fitting

(i)   Open out the two front leg pieces and place right side up. Place the two front yoke sections in position, right side down, match fitting lines and tack yoke seams. (Fig. 1.)

Tacking
for fitting

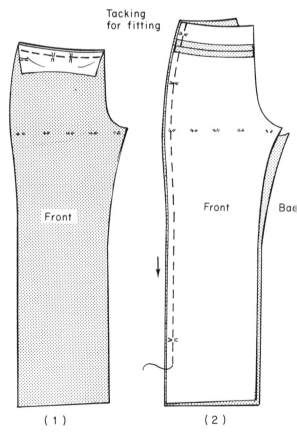

(1)   (2)

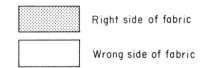

(ii)   Tack back yokes to back legs.

(iii)   Lay back legs on table right side up and place front legs on top right side down. Lift and match up side seams. Tack from waist to hem. Leave 23cm (9in.) open at left side of left leg. (Fig. 2.)

(iv)   Move front trouser piece over so that inside leg seams match. Tack from crutch to hem. (Fig. 3.)

(v)   You can't begin to fit trousers if they drag on the floor so turn up each hem on fitting line and hold with a row of large basting stitches. (Fig. 4.)

slightly towards the front. This takes the side seam further back which keeps it out of sight when the trousers are seen from the front.

(i)   Fold each leg right side out with the inside leg seam 1·3cm ($\frac{1}{2}$in.) nearer the front than the outside leg seam.

(ii)   Arrange the seams in position at the hem and make sure they remain 1·3cm ($\frac{1}{2}$in.) apart right up to the crutch. Don't try to smooth out the whole leg. The shape at the inside leg and at the crutch will appear as fullness in that area and as you press you will find that the sections that matter; the creases, will flatten out anyway. (Fig. 5.)

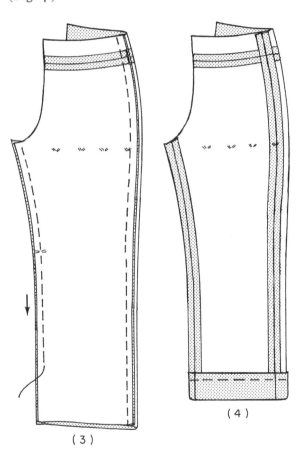

(3)

(4)

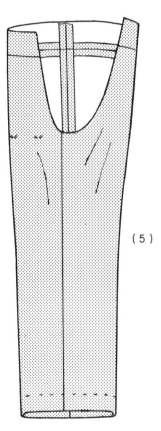

(5)

Pressing

The creases must be put in before fitting, they improve the appearance, but also hang better. Trousers hang better if the inside leg seam is

(iii)   It is much easier to press on a table or surface large enough to take the whole leg but if you have to use the ironing board place the bottom section of leg on the board and fold the waist part over at the top so that it doesn't hang over the edge. Settle the hem and front crease, the back crease automatically finds its position.

(iv) Wring out your muslin and spread it over the lower 30cm (12in.) of the front of the leg. Press the front crease in working up the leg from the hem (Fig. 6). Lift the cloth and if the fabric

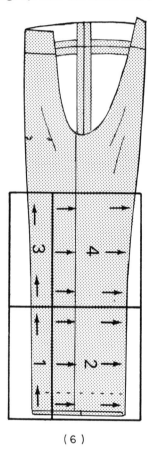

(6)

is smooth, press again. Lift cloth and press a third time. Move cloth to cover whole width of leg and press from front crease across leg to back. Lift cloth and look underneath. If all is well, press again and then again.

Press the next 30cm (12in.) of front crease and then press across to the back.

Arrange the top part of the front crease up to the yoke join (you can put the creases up through the yoke after fitting), press, but this time do not press across to the back. Instead, press the inside

leg seam from where previous pressing finished, up to the crutch, stretching the seam a little as you do it.

You can now smooth out the remainder of the back crease. This should finish at the waist exactly at the centre back, but as with the front crease, don't press up through the yoke at this stage.

Hang up both legs to cool and dry.

First fitting

Slip on the right leg only and hold it up, using the curved petersham fitting aid (*see page* 78). Make sure the crutch is as high as it will go and then check the width of the leg at thigh level, knee level and at the hem (Fig. 7). Turn sideways and

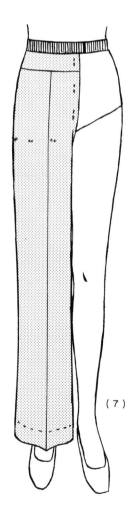

(7)

see if they look the correct width. Don't worry at this stage about any excess fullness there may be above the thigh line.

Remove leg and re-tack if necessary, letting out or taking in the required amount. Try on again to check. This is not a final decision about width, it is simply that your first complete fitting will now be unhampered by bagginess or tightness in the lower part of the leg.

Tacking both legs together

For added strength on larger sizes, run another row of tacking up the outside leg, through the turnings to form a welt seam. On the left leg turn under the front seam allowance where the zip will go, and tack. (Fig. 8.)

Place the two inside leg seams right sides together and tack from there up to the front waist. Turn the trousers round and tack from crutch up to back waist. (Fig. 9.)

Welt seam

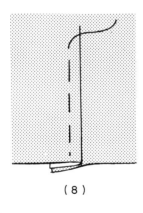

(8)

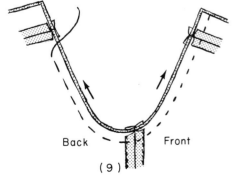

Back   Front

(9)

Second fitting

Wear a waist length top or sweater. Put the trousers on and put the correct shoes on. Pin up the side opening and hold up the trousers with your curved petersham fitting aid. (Fig. 10a.)

Pull the trousers up all round, and up to the crutch as high as they will go, and then gently ease them down again at the side seams until there are no creases running up from the front crutch and the line from the crutch to the side seam is straight.

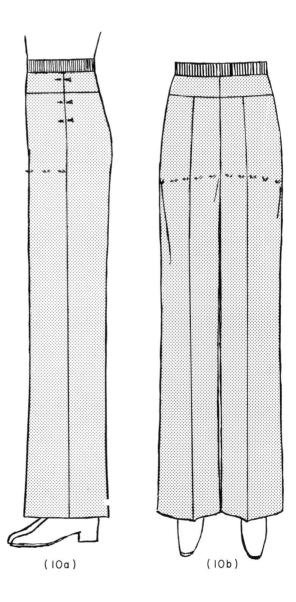

(10a)   (10b)

Now stand still and look at the front. Then look at the back. Finally turn to the side and look at the run of the side seam; this may be running towards the back from thigh up to the waist, or occasionally to the front. The crutch line marked on the front should be horizontal. If it runs down at the sides it indicates either that the back trouser must be lifted into the yoke seam or the front crutch must be lowered. Then the trousers need either dropping at the side or else the front crutch needs loosening or lifting. (Fig. 10b.)

Identify and correct all other faults first and if by correcting them you do not correct this side seam line, then examine the trousers again to see which alteration above will straighten it.

Try to identify the faults you see from the following list. Most alterations involve lifting at some point so you can check whether you have identified the problem by pinching the fabric and lifting at the appropriate point to see if it cures the trouble. With most trouser alterations you will have to take them off, re-tack, and put them on again before you can be sure that you are doing the right thing.

Fitting faults

Fault	*Cause and solution*
(i) Horizontal creases across front at crutch	Crutch seam too curved, snip at front and you will see how it opens up. Take off and re-tack (Fig. 11).
(ii) Folds running up to crutch on front and back, also possibly waist dipping at back	Basin of crutch seam too narrow. Let out back extension and also a little on front (Fig. 12).
(iii) Thigh bulge at front or side	Trouser too tight. Let out at inside leg – if you let out sides it will emphasize the problem (Fig. 13).
(iv) Baggy folds below a well fitting seat	Crutch seam not shaped enough. Scoop out more under the leg; do not take any off fork or hip level. After doing this you will be able to lift them higher at the waist, take in at the yoke seam (Fig. 14).
(v) Legs twisting below thigh level	(a) Trousers pulled up too high, either let down at waist or let out crutch extension (Fig. 15). (b) Wrong width of front leg compared with back for the figure. If seams twist to the front then either take in the back seam or let out the front. If they twist to the back, take in back seam or let out front seam. If in doubt, unpick lower part of seam while trousers are being worn, let fabric hang and you will soon see whether you have to fill in a gap or take away an overlapping surplus.
(vi) Surplus fabric above hips. Trousers too high at waist or folds across back waist	Trouser too long from waist to crutch. Take out in yoke seam. Can be caused by hollow back in which case remove yoke and set on a little lower. You may also have to take a little in at the CB seam to make waist fit (Fig. 16).

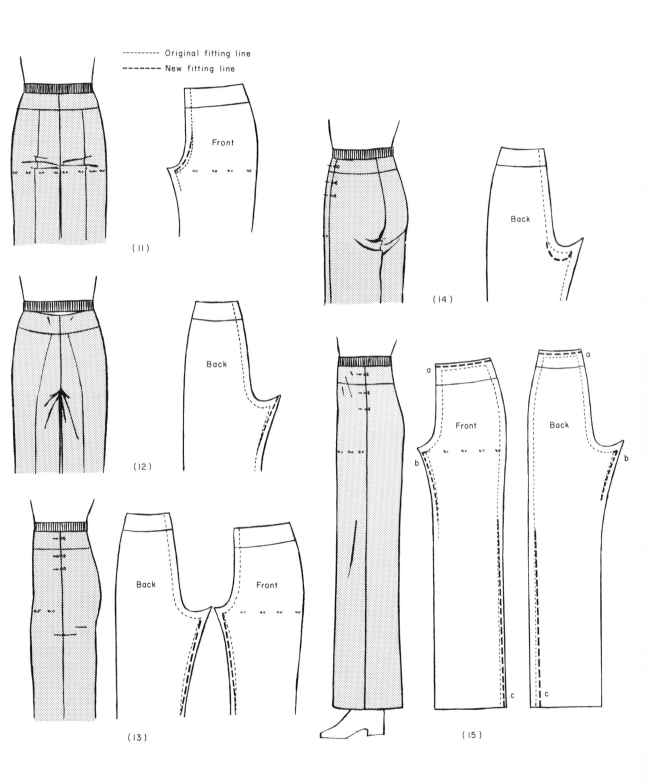

---------- Original fitting line
━━━━━ New fitting line

Front

(11)

Back

(12)

Back   Front

(13)

Back

(14)

a   a
Front   Back
b   b
c   c

(15)

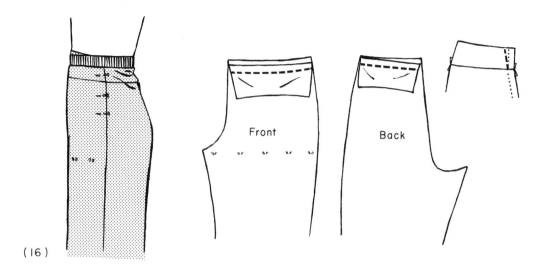

(16)

After each fitting mark the alteration on both halves of each piece. Tack up and try on again. Sometimes correcting one fault will reveal another so it is wise not to do any machining until you are satisfied with the fit. After marking all the new seam lines, take the trousers apart.

Making trousers
The zip is inserted in the side seam in these instructions but you can equally well put it at the centre front if you prefer. Never put it in the centre back or it prevents that seam from giving and providing room to move.

Reinforcing the front seam
Although you want the back seam to stretch, the front seam should be held firmly in place. There are two ways of doing this and the choice depends on fabric being used. On jersey where there is liable to be a good deal of give in wear, tack a length of seam binding or pre-shrunk tape on the fitting line, on one front trouser only, on the wrong side. Also tack a piece about 10cm (4in.) long from the crutch down the inside leg to prevent this part from stretching. Later when the seam is stitched the machining will go through the tape. (Figs. 17a&b.)

If your fabric is firm there will be no need to reinforce the whole seam but only the curved

Reinforcing

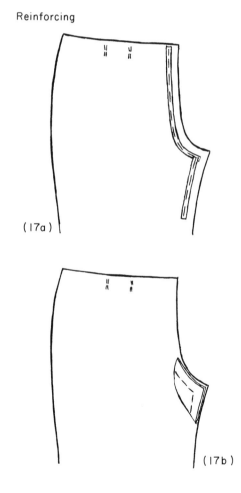

(17a)

(17b)

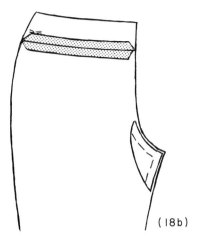

section at the base, and the inside leg. This can be done with tape as described above, or with a triangle of lining fabric.

Cut two 10cm (4in.) squares of lining or cotton fabric. Fold into a triangle and place on the trouser fork, on the wrong side of both the front leg sections so that the two straight edges run along the inside leg seam and the crutch seam. The fold is on the cross and will stretch as you tack it in place. This will be held in place later by machining.

If your fabric is a pale colour or there is the least chance that this piece of fabric will show, use the tape method.

If you are putting the zip in the centre front seam, this will act as reinforcement but you will still have to put a stay in the lower part by one of these methods.

Yoke seams

(i) Place each yoke section to the correct leg piece, matching fitting lines carefully and easing the curved edges together. If you need to pin, place a couple across the seam. Tack and machine. (Fig. 18a.)

(ii) Remove tacks, trim turnings and snip. Press joins open using sleeve board or pressing pad. Trim ends of turning off at an angle. (Fig. 18b.)

Leg seams

Arrange each leg on the table with the waist at the right.

(i) Place front and back leg sections together matching up the fitting lines on the outside leg seam. Place the yoke seams together carefully and put in a pin, across the seam to hold. This pin will remain in position until after the seam has been machined. Tack the right leg from waist to hem (Fig. 19a). On the left leg place the zip against the seam with the metal tag 6mm ($\frac{1}{4}$in.) below the fitting line (or more if the fabric is particularly thick). Make a chalk mark to indicate the length of the zip, just above the end

Yoke seams

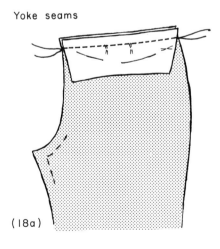

(18a)

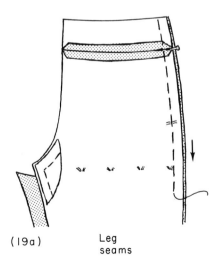

(19a)   Leg seams

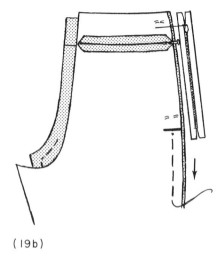

(19b)

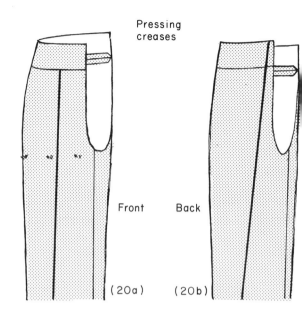

Pressing
creases

Front   Back

(20a)   (20b)

stop. Leave the pin in position at the yoke and
tack from the chalk mark to the hem. (Fig. 19b.)
(ii)   Swing the legs round and arrange the inside
leg fitting lines together, lifting the front leg over
until the raw edges are together. Begin tacking at
the crutch working down to the hem. There will
be a little ease to cope with between the crutch
and thigh line but when tacking be sure to keep
the crutch line straight.
(iii)   Machine these four seams from top to hem,
moving gently over the pin at the yoke. Remove
tacks. Press seams open on a sleeve board, working from top to hem for as much of the seam as
you can.
(iv)   Trim the raw edges down to 1·3cm ($\frac{1}{2}$in.)
and neaten by zig-zag or hand overcasting.
Neaten the section where the zip is to go up as
far as the yoke seam.

Press the creases

Now that fitting is complete and seams are
finished, press in the creases in their permanent
position. Arrange each leg as before and press in
the same way, but more firmly this time and
taking the crease right up through the yoke to
the waist. (Fig. 20a&b.)

The front creases should come about 6·0–7·5cm
($2\frac{1}{2}$–3in.) either side of the centre front, running
almost parallel with the front seam. The exact
distance here varies with the figure but it is not

particularly slimming to have the creases too far
apart.

At the back the crease must finish exactly at the
centre back.

Press well and hang to dry before going on to
the next stage.

Zip

Insert the zip following the instructions on page
93.

Crutch seam

Turn the legs right side out.
(i)   Put the two inside leg seams together. Insert
one pin across the seam and leave in place until
after machining.
(ii)   Put yoke seams together on the front and
on the back and insert a pin in the same way.
(iii)   Tack from crutch round to front waist,
return to crutch and tack from there up to the
back waist, tacking through the reinforcement.
(Fig. 21.)
(iv)   Machine this seam, either using a slight
zig-zag stitch or pulling the work very slightly as
it goes under the needle. Work a second row of
machining on the section right under the leg, for
strength. Stitch slowly over the pins. (Fig. 22.)

Crutch seam

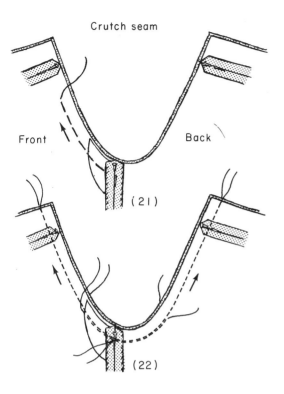

Front   Back

(21)

(22)

Waist finish

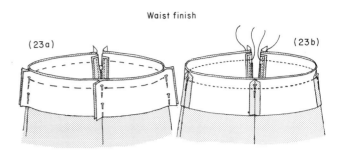

(23a)   (23b)

(v) Remove tacking stitches. Press this seam flat first slightly stretching the section from the waist down for about 15cm (6in.) to eliminate any puckering.

(vi) Press the seam open from front and back waist down to where it begins to curve. Round the curved part use only the toe of the iron to smooth it, don't attempt to open the turnings. The trousers will hang better if this section of seam is left standing up.

(vii) Trim raw edges to 1·3cm ($\frac{1}{2}$in.) and neaten.

Waist finish

(i) Pin yoke facings in position right side down to right side of trouser. Tack the fitting lines together but leave the end of each piece free to allow the joins to be made. Pin raw edges of facing together (or press back if using turning). Tack and machine the joins and press open. Trim raw edges to 6mm ($\frac{1}{4}$in.). Trim away end of turnings at an angle. (Figs.23a&b.)

(ii) Place a pin across each join to hold and machine round the waist edge, working from the trouser side, not the facing side. Stitch across the top of the zip, including the zip tape. (Fig. 23b.) If fabric is inclined to stretch, stitch a length of seam binding or tape into the waist.

(iii) Remove tacks, trim one turning to 6mm ($\frac{1}{4}$in.) and the facing turning to a little less. If you want a firmer waist edge, stitch a length of curved petersham, into the join, hemming it or machining it to the turnings.

You can also, if you wish, work a row of machining through the facing and the turnings to keep the facing well over to the wrong side (24a).

(iv) Roll the top edge join slightly to the wrong side of the trousers and tack. Press. (Fig. 24b.)

(v) Turn under the raw edges beside the zip, trimming away as much bulk of turning inside as possible.

(vi) Neaten the lower raw edge of the facing, trimming it if necessary, so that it just covers the yoke seam. Tack down along the seam. (Fig. 24b.)

Waist finish

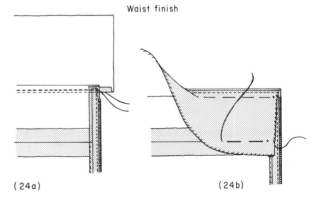

(24a)   (24b)

(vii) Hem the ends by the zip and prick stitch by hand or else machine through the yoke join to hold the facing down. Work from right side for this.

(viii)   You will probably find a hook at the top of the zip quite useful to help take the strain when fastening the zip, especially if the trousers are a close fit.

Use a large hook and an eye, size 2 or 3. Sew the hook in position first, holding the head down initially with about 6 or 8 very strong stitches, then work round each eye with close buttonhole stitch.

Fasten the eye over the hook, close the zip and position the eye, using a pin to hold it. Sew it on firmly with close buttonhole stitch. (Fig. 25.)

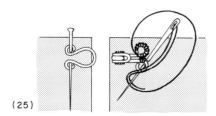

(25)

Hems (Also see page 104)
(i)   Run the iron over the creases for about 5cm (2in.) not to remove altogether but just enough to make it easier to turn up.
(ii)   Turn up and tack the bottom fold, check that the two inside legs seams are equal in length
(iii)   Trim away seam turnings inside hem. Trim down to 4cm ($1\frac{1}{2}$in.) hem depth and neaten raw edge. (Fig. 26.)

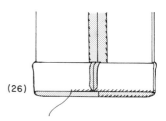

(26)

(iv)   Slip Wundaweb under edge, making sure it is covered. Press with damp muslin round inside of leg on hem turning, taking care not to stretch the trouser. Turn to right side and press again.

Final press
(i)   Slide waist onto sleeve board and press area from waist downwards.
(ii)   Arrange each leg in turn on the table and re-press the creases, working especially firmly where the hem has just been turned up.
(iii)   Hang trousers up to cool for several hours before wearing.

SECTION 2

EQUIPMENT, PRESSING, AND MAKING UP THE BASIC PATTERNS

I

Equipment

Some of the problems encountered in sewing, especially by the less experienced dressmakers, are completely eliminated once the right tools are used. The following lists include the essential items and also some extras which merely make the job easier.

The only large items of equipment you need are a table for cutting out (or you can use a cutting board which you can put anywhere) and, of course, a sewing machine. All the other things you need are comparatively inexpensive.

For measuring

1 Tape measure
The most useful tape for some time to come is one with inches on one side and metric measurements on the reverse. Buy a firm, fibre glass, tape with metal ends and clear figures.

2 Ruler
A foot ruler is a little short for most flat measurements; buy an 18 inch or yard stick, or the metric equivalents.

3 Gauge
There are two useful ones, the six inch metal one with red moveable marker, and a little shaped gauge made by Milward's which has edges cut to a variety of widths up to 5cm (2in.).

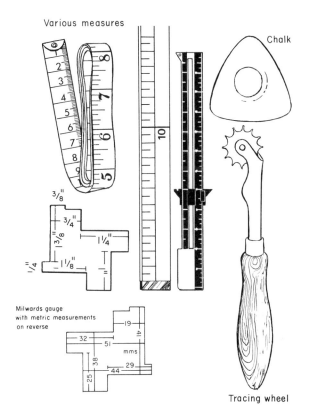

Various measures

Chalk

3/8"

3/4"
3/8"
1/4"
1/4"
1 1/4"
1 1/8"

Milwards gauge with metric measurements on reverse

19
41
32
51
mms
38
29
25
44

Tracing wheel

Waist marker

Marking

(a) Tailor's Chalk
Buy at least half a dozen pieces of white. Keep them well sharpened, using your scissors opened out. The coloured chalks are inclined to leave marks on some fabrics so white is safest and it shows up on most fabrics, appearing as a dull line on white fabrics.

(b) Tracing Wheel
Make sure the teeth are sharp when you choose it. Use it for tracing off patterns onto paper and for marking the wrong side of fabric with carbon paper.

Cutting

(a) Scissors
You need three pairs: a small pair for snipping threads and turnings, blades about 4cm ($1\frac{1}{2}$in.) long (shorter blades reduce their usefulness to only thread-snipping as the blades will not bite on fabric); a medium-sized pair with 20cm (4in.) or 22cm ($4\frac{1}{2}$in.) blades, and shaped handle for comfort, for trimming raw edges and all cutting jobs that are not snipping; cutting out shears also with shaped handles to put your whole hand in and flat to rest on the table, blades about 15cm (6in.) to 7·5cm (7in.) long. Cutting out is much easier with large scissors.

Scissors should be of good quality steel, and a well-known make such as Wilkinson or Taylor's. If you can go to a tailors' supply shop you will get the best ones available. When they need sharpening, that is when cutting becomes hard work, take them to a cutler rather than to the man who has called to sharpen the lawnmower.

(b) Unpicker
This is a useful tool to have for cutting machine-made buttonholes. It can be hazardous using it for unpicking, in case it slips. Use small scissors for this.

(c) Machine needles
Plain, ball point, spear point.

Equipment

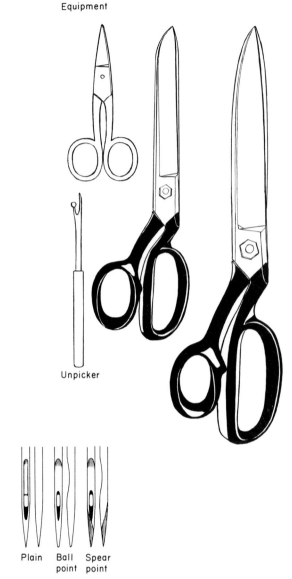

Unpicker

Plain   Ball   Spear
        point point

Machine needles very much
enlarged

Handsewing

(a) Needles
Buy several packets of Betweens, in assorted sizes, or a packet of each size from 6 up to 9. Betweens are short, with the normal eye. Hand

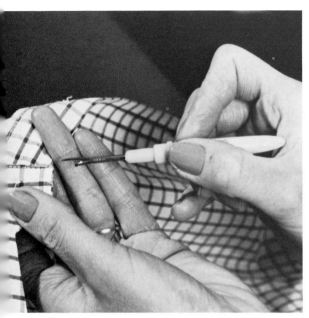

6 *Unpicking a seam (courtesy Dritz Ltd)*

sewing is much easier with these than with the long Sharps needle because your fingers are nearer to the point and therefore you have more control, and also you can make much smaller, more even stitches.

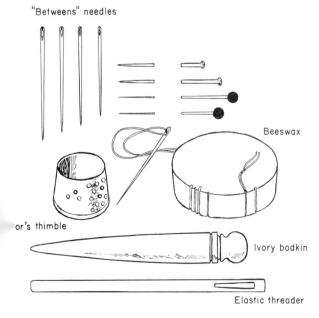

"Betweens" needles

Beeswax

or's thimble

Ivory bodkin

Elastic threader

(b) Thimble
A thimble is vital to good comfortable hand sewing. A dome thimble, whether metal, plastic, or even silver, is uncomfortable to wear because it keeps out the air. To wear one for an hour is equivalent to wearing Elastoplast for several days. Small wonder that so many people say they cannot wear them. In addition the unfilled end hampers your work, rather like wearing shoes that are too big. Buy a tailor's steel thimble with an open end. The tip of your finger should be level with the end of the thimble.

(c) Pins
Buy a couple of boxes of steel pins. If you can obtain the long ones these are very useful when cutting out. A few of those with coloured plastic heads are useful when fitting a garment in a thick loosely woven material as you can see them easily. If you tip pins into a bowl for use, remember to put the piece of rust preventive paper in with them.

(d) Beeswax
For strengthening threads before sewing on buttons; helps to smooth out twisting threads; can be run over the teeth of metal zips if they stick. Also, when sewing with double thread run it through wax to prevent the two threads from parting as you sew.

(e) Bodkin
A plastic or bone bodkin is for removing tacking stitches quickly and without harming the fabric. Particularly useful when pulling basting from mounted garments.

(f) Elastic Threader
You will need one of these or a big metal bodkin with an eye, for turning rouleau.

Threads
(a) Tacking thread. For tailor tacks and for all tacking. It is soft and breaks easily without harming the fabric. You can break it with your fingers which saves time. It is fluffy and so does not slip when in place.

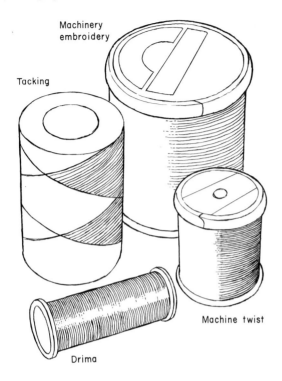

Machinery embroidery

Tacking

Machine twist

Drima

(b)   Sewing thread. You soon acquire a collection of colours. Use for all machining and hand sewing but not for tacking as it is too strong, it slips, and dark colours can leave fluff in pale fabrics. Coats' Drima is fine but strong and is easy to match up because the thread sinks well into the fabric rather than remaining on the surface. Cut the end for threading, breaking tends to fray the end.

(c)   In addition, buy at some time a big reel of Anchor Machine Embroidery thread and use it for mounting stitches on fine material such as chiffon, silk, etc.

Machining

Additional feet, etc., will be provided with your machine. Keep them near you. If you put them away you tend not to make use of them.

Make sure you keep a duster, oil, and brush nearby too. When sewing, particularly on synthetics, you frequently need to uncover the spool area and brush out fluff. Put one drop of oil in your machine quite often.

Keep plenty of machine needles of all sizes and all types, including ball-point for synthetic jersey and spear-ended for leather and suede, as well as the special varieties for tacking etc. As

7   *Sewing thread (courtesy J. & P. Coates Ltd)*

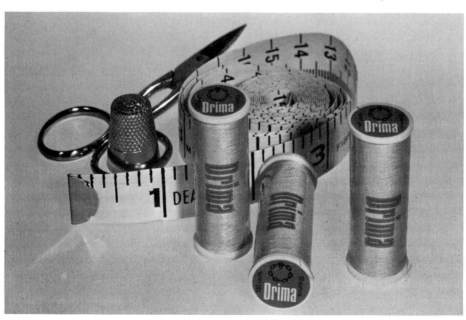

with the feet, keep the box near the machine so that you have no excuse for machining with a blunt needle.

Pressing

If you can organize a table with a blanket on it and a piece of sheeting this is best for pressing as it gives you a bigger surface for supporting the work. However, an ironing board may have to suffice and if this is so remember to support big pieces of soft fabric by placing a chair or clothes horse beneath the board.

(a) Sleeve board

This is used for all pressing of sewing processes. It is seldom, if ever, used for pressing sleeves. To press well you work on a very small area at a time and this is one advantage of the sleeve board as it immediately draws your attention to that part only. It also enables you to press shaped areas such as darts and curved seams without flattening them, by using the end of the board. Finally the board raises the work to a much better working height.

Stand it on the table or on the ironing board.

A tailor's sleeve board is best, although expensive. It has two sides to it and all four ends are rounded at different sizes so you have a choice of two widths and four ends depending on the size and nature of the part you are pressing.

(b) Pressing cloth

You need two pieces of muslin because some fabrics need a damp and a dry cloth. Buy 1 metre (1¼yds) and cut it in half to make two manageable pieces. Muslin can be wrung out until nearly dry for light fabrics, made damper for medium ones, and folded over if more moisture is required. With such a variety of fibres and textures available now, and with fewer heavy worsteds and tweeds, muslin is much more useful, and safer, than calico.

(c) Irons

Two irons are the ideal, a steam iron which can also be used when necessary with a dry or damp muslin, and a fairly heavy ordinary iron with a small base for pressing heavier fabrics, putting in pleats, creases in trousers, etc. This is always used with a damp muslin, sometimes also using a dry one afterwards.

One of the limitations of the steam iron is that the amount of steam is constant and cannot usually be varied to suit the fabric, and by the

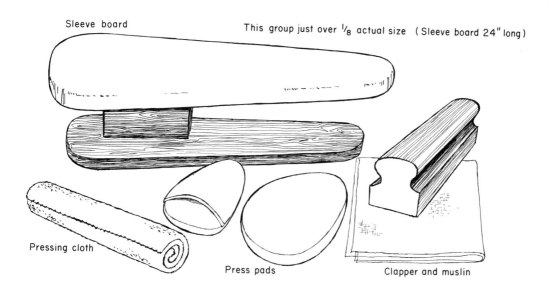

Sleeve board   This group just over ⅛ actual size (Sleeve board 24" long)

Pressing cloth

Press pads

Clapper and muslin

8   *A general purpose dry iron*

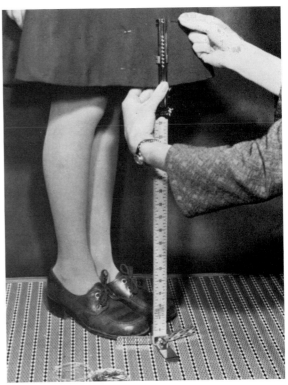

9   *Hem marker (courtesy Dritz Ltd)*

time you have waited for more steam the base of the iron has left an imprint. Sunbeam Electric, however, make a steam iron with a steam button on top which when pressed spurts an extra and forceful jet of steam onto the fabric. This can be directed exactly where you want it and you can also vary the amount according to the needs of the material.

(d) Pressing block
This is used for banging in steam, after removing damp muslin, for setting pleats and creases and is also useful on stubborn springy synthetics.

(e) Pressing Pads
You may like to buy or make a few pads of different shapes for shoulders, sleeves, etc., but a small turkish towel folded or rolled is a good substitute.

Equipment for fitting
(a)   Small scissors for snipping tacks.
(b)   Pins. In lacey or loosely woven fabrics, use the long pins with coloured plastic heads as they are easier to locate later.
(c)   Tape measure.
(d)   Sharp chalk.
(e)   Hem marker. A ruler screwed to a firm block of wood or a purchased marker.
(f)   Waist marker. This is useful for checking the waist position on dresses and also for holding up skirts and trousers at the fitting, before the waist is finished. Take a waist length plus 7cm (3in.) of curved petersham, sew a short piece of Velcro to one end, either hemming it or machining it in place. Put the petersham round your waist over your dress, pull it fairly tight, but not to wrinkle the garment, mark the overlap with a pin. Sew the corresponding piece of Velcro in position.

2

Pressing

There is no doubt that pressing is the most important aspect of sewing. If your machining and hand sewing are not up to standard no one will know provided you are sensible and refrain from doing any on the outside of the garment. If you haven't conquered fitting, you can choose flat garments, wrap-round styles, etc., for a while. But work will always look glaringly unfinished if it has not been pressed correctly and yet it isn't a technique you can learn beforehand.

Let us look at what is involved. First, it is not ironing, it is not smoothing wrinkles by sliding the iron about. Ironing is comparatively easy because the garment has already been made and shaped and put in place.

When making something you take a piece of material that has been woven or knitted quite flat and you shape it into a garment by cutting it into smaller pieces and rejoining it. You also hope, by the use of darts, actually to create bulges. The fabric will not take kindly to this so you have to encourage it with the use of heat, pressure and moisture to change direction at seams and folds.

Not only do materials respond differently to this treatment according to their fibre content, thickness and construction, but they need the three vital commodities in varying amounts. This is really what pressing is about – learning just how much moisture is needed and for how long, how hot the iron should be *combined with the moisture* and exactly how you should apply the iron – short sharp dabs, heavy bangs and how

many of them. You have to learn too, how to use your other hand for stretching and smoothing. Finally, you have to learn what treatment is needed afterwards – hanging to cool, drying off with the iron, alone or with a dry cloth etc.

Machining, too, has to be taken into account because before you can start to press a process you have to smooth out the stitches. You have sandwiched two or more layers together under pressure and used two threads joined in between and it is essential to press it into the fabric before attempting to make the fabric do what you want. Hand sewing fortunately is softer and under less tension, so it doesn't, or shouldn't, disturb the material as much. Hand sewing will be pressed, of course, but only for the sake of appearance if the stitches show.

It is impossible to give rules for pressing any material in detail except under fibre headings such as wool, nylon, cotton, etc., because it is necessary to know what thickness, what weave, what finish etc., is involved. Some detailed hints are given for each fabric in each section, but remember that the technique of superb pressing is only acquired with a lot of practice.

2.1 Directions for machining and pressing seams

The finished effect on seams will be improved if sewing and pressing is done working from the widest part to the narrowest on each section of

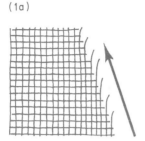

(1a)

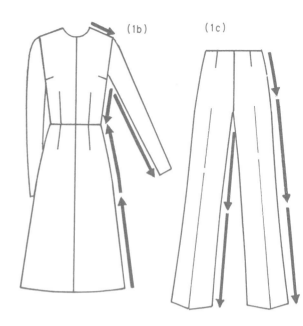

(1b)   (1c)

garment. On woven fabrics this is working with the fibres as they fray off rather than against them. Try fraying off the edge of a piece of fabric cut on the bias and you will see that the fibres lie in one direction. Stitch with them and the tendency to puckering is reduced (Fig. 1a).

When pressing, work along the seam in the same direction to avoid a dragged down effect on skirts. With trousers, press from waist to hem to avoid them looking pulled up at the ankles. With short seams such as shoulders it helps to prevent stretching to press in the correct direction.

Some fabrics such as velvet need special treatment, but this is dealt with under the appropriate later sections.

Correct direction (Fig. 1b&c)

Skirt seams:	hem up to waist
Bodice seams:	underarm to waist
Shoulder seams:	neck to shoulder
Sleeve seams:	underarm to wrist
Trousers:	waist to hem

3

Making up the basic dress

3.1 Darts

(i) Fold the fabric wrong side out and match up the markings. It will be easier to do this if you have used tailor tacks as you can roll the two layers of fabric between your fingers until you can feel the two sets of tailor tacks are together.

(ii) If you need to hold it with pins before tacking, use no more than 3, putting one across the end, one below the point and one half way (Fig. 1a).

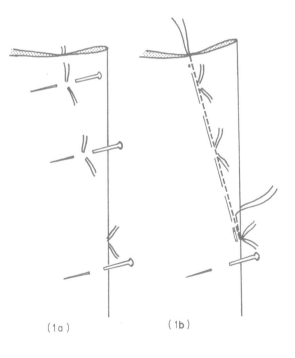

(1a)   (1b)

(iii) Start tacking at the raw edges and work towards the point. Finish with one back stitch just short of the end of the dart. Leave the last pin in place as it will help to keep the fabric flat while you machine (Fig. 1b). Some people prefer to remove tailor tacks at this stage but I prefer to use them as a guide, ending my row of machining exactly on the last tailor tack instead of trampling tacking into the fabric. It helps, in addition, to measure off pairs of darts putting a chalk mark at the exact point of the dart, to ensure that they are the same length. You can also draw a straight chalk line to stitch on if the dart is completely straight.

(iv) Put the work under the machine with the bulk of it to the left and starting at the raw edge, lower the foot at an angle so that it is pointing towards the end of the dart. Turn the wheel towards you until the needle is in the work. Reverse if you like to fasten off this way and then machine carefully to the point. If you reverse to fasten off make sure you stitch in the fold of the dart.

(v) Remove tacks by pulling the knot. Remove tailor tacks and the pin. Snip ends of thread close to fabric.

(vi) Place dart flat on sleeve board and press the stitching to smooth it.

(vii) If the fabric is thin open out the work and place it on the sleeve board so that the point is level with the end of the board and the fabric of the dart is standing upright. Press dart over so that it is flat. You will probably be using a steam iron on a light fabric. Having pressed it in the correct direction, which is so that the bulk of the fabric is towards the centre of the garment, or in the case of horizontal bust darts, downwards to the waist, now press it again really well, pressing only up to the end of the stitching. By arranging the dart on the sleeve board you can ensure that you don't flatten the shaping that the dart is providing in the fabric.

(viii)   Turn the work over and press again on the right side.

(ix)   In all medium and heavy weight fabrics the dart should be split open and trimmed to reduce bulk, but remember that all fitting must have been completed before any cutting away is done (Figs. 2a&b).

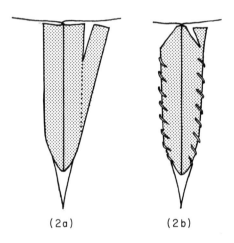

(2a)   (2b)

After pressing the stitching, split the dart along the fold nearly to the end. Trim away a little of the fabric. Open the work and press the dart open instead of to one side, taking great care with the point, which should be flattened. You will be using a damp muslin to press these fabrics so drape a corner of it over the toe of the iron and work carefully, continually looking under the cloth to make quite certain all is well. You may have some additional pressing to do on the right side with this type of dart.

After the fabric is cool, neaten the raw edges by hand overcasting, or by zig-zag stitch.

(x)   Trim off the raw edges at an angle to reduce bulk, before proceeding to the next stage.

3.2 Open seams

Sometimes called a plain seam, this is used more often than any other because it is suitable for all fabrics and it is flat. Other types of seam are described later where they are suggested for particular outfits.

Making an open seam

(i)   Place one piece of fabric on the table, right side uppermost. Place second piece of fabric on top, right side down. Raw edges should be nearest to you.

(ii)   Line up the two seam lines by lifting and re-spreading, not by dragging. It is easier to do this if you have used tailor tacks because you can feel those on the lower piece of fabric with your forefinger while moving the top fabric into position.

(iii)   It is best not to use any pins as they lift the material, but if your fabric is particularly obstinate place a few pins down the length of the seam, inserting them across the seam to avoid disturbing the fabric too much (Fig. 3a).

(iv)   Use a long piece of tacking thread and a needle one size larger than for hand sewing on the particular type of fabric; put a knot in the end and begin tacking, picking up small amounts of fabric on the needle (Fig. 3b).

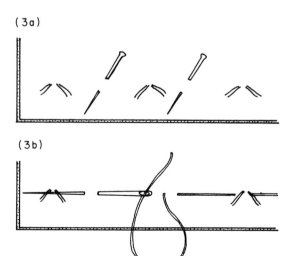

(3a)

(3b)

(v)   At the end of the seam pull the fabric to loosen the tacking thread slightly, this will help to avoid a puckered seam, and fasten off.

(vi)   On long straight seams it may help to rule a chalk line before machining, to give you a guide line. Many people remove their tailor tacks at this stage but as they were the first marks to be put in they are the most accurate, so I prefer to leave them in and use them as a guide rather than the tacking.

(vii)   Place work under machine with raw edges to the right, lower the foot onto the fabric, turn the wheel until the needle is in the work, and machine, reversing for 6mm ($\frac{1}{4}$in.) if you like this method of finishing the end.

(viii)   Fasten off at the end by reversing or sew in all machine ends, after removing work from machine.

(ix)   Remove tacking by grasping the knot, use your bodkin for difficult stitches. Remove tailor tacks, using tweezers (or teeth) for difficult ones.

Pressing

(i)   Press the stitching flat to remove puckers and to help to embed the thread in the fabric. Use damp muslin and medium-hot iron, or steam iron if that is best for your fabric.

(ii)   Open the garment out over your sleeve board, arranging one short length of seam in position if it is a long one. Open the end of the seam with your fingers and then, holding a corner of the damp muslin in one hand and the iron in the other, open the seam by pressing on the cloth with the toe of the iron. Work your way along to the end of the sleeveboard in this way, making sharp pressing movements (Fig. 4).

(iii)   Lift the cloth and examine the seam. Correct any wrinkles by pressing again.

(iv)   Press the whole section again, more boldly this time to set the fabric in its new position. Leave to cool.

(v)   Move the work along and press another section in the same way taking care not to leave a mark where the sleeveboard ends.

(vi)   Turn the work over and press the right side, still using the cloth but with less pressure than you extended on the wrong side. Leave to cool.

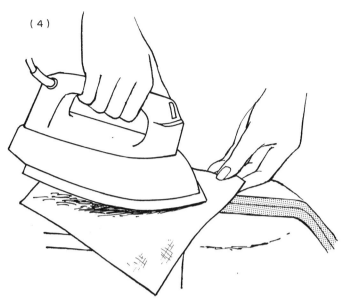

(4)

(vii)   Using medium scissors, trim back the turnings at an angle to reduce bulk before you proceed to the next seam.

10   An open seam, neatened with zig-zag stitch (courtesy Bernina Sewing Machines Ltd)

Neatening an open seam

Always stitch and press seams before neatening, otherwise an ugly ridge may show through when you press. Some fabrics such as knitteds, bonded fabrics, etc., do not, strictly speaking, need neatening because they do not fray. However, you may feel as I do, that you should do it as a point of honour so that the wrong side of the garment will stand examination just the same as the right side. Also some knitted fabrics tend to curl up at the edges and neatening helps to keep them flat.

Fraying fabrics

Work a row of straight machine stitching 1·3cm (½in.) from the seam line; it helps to chalk a straight line, otherwise use machine foot as a guide. Trim fabric, using medium scissors, a few centimetres (inches) at a time, and overcast (Fig. 5). Work from left to right taking the needle

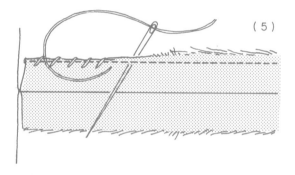

(5)

under the machine stitches and pulling the thread quite tight to compress the narrow raw edge, and hold the fraying fibre firmly down. If possible, work in the direction the fibres lie so that you flatten them as you work.

Press the stitching to finish, pulling the edge slightly to remove any tightness that has been caused by the stitching.

This is an excellent finish, though time consuming, and can be used on any weight of material.

Slightly fraying fabrics

Either overcast by hand (you can't pull the thread too tight as there is no holding stitch) or zig-zag by machine. Test your fabric first if you zig-zag and find the most suitable size and width of stitch. A big zig-zag will not prevent fraying as the fibres come away between the stitches. Adjust the stitch to the shortest narrowest stitch you can work effectively on the fabric. With some lightweight fabrics the edge curls over if the stitch is too wide, and if it is too long it can easily draw it up.

After setting the stitch, trim the raw edges cleanly, using medium scissors, and stitch in the correct direction to avoid further fraying.

If your material frays but you are determined not to do any hand sewing you can combine both methods, working a row of straight machining first and then a zig-zag over it.

Non-fraying fabrics

These can have a zig-zag stitch on them but it is unnecessary and it uses a lot of thread. Instead use the blind hem stitch, No. I stitch on the Bernina, worked just within a cleanly cut raw edge (Fig. 6). The single zig-zag stitch helps to hold the turnings flat.

(6)

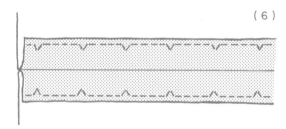

Pinking shears

There is little point in using pinking shears; if your fabric frays it will go on fraying but shorter fibres will come off. If the fabric does not fray at all it is time consuming to do all that trimming and you are also reducing your turnings to a dangerously small amount.

Binding

This adds bulk and it takes a long time to do properly. Machining both sides for instance, makes it very rigid and hard. Confine this finish to armholes on fine fabrics and decorative edging.

3.3 Facings

Applying a facing to an edge is one method of neatening it. The facing is fairly wide, from 4cm ($1\frac{1}{2}$in.) up to about 10cm (4in.) according to the position, so it is useful in places where the inside of the garment might be visible, e.g. neckline, armholes.

Fit the garment first and make any adjustments, then cut the facing to fit the edge. If there are seams in the garment it may be necessary to make corresponding joins in the facing, e.g. shoulders.

The facing is usually left hanging loose inside the garment because if stitched down, however carefully, it can then be seen from the right side. If there is another layer of fabric, for example mounting, or the turnings of a seam, the facing can be caught down in places; but a better, and quite invisible method of preventing it from popping out in wear is to slip small pieces of Wundaweb between facing and garment, pressing to hold in place.

For a decorative effect the facing can be turned over onto the right side of the garment and stitched down (Fig. 7).

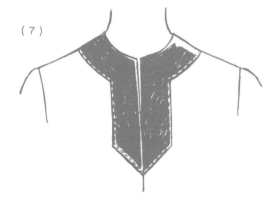

(7)

Facing the neck of the basic dress

(i)   Cut out the facing. It is not absolutely necessary to tailor tack the turnings. The correct neckline should by now be clearly marked on the garment so you can use that as a stitching guide. Do not interface a facing and do not mount it unless it is a very flimsy fabric such as chiffon.

(ii)   Place front and back neck facings in position, making sure the centre back edge comes well over the zip edge. Pin.

(iii)   Slide shoulder of dress onto sleeve board and fold back the two ends of facing at the shoulder seams (Fig. 8). Crease with the iron so that the two folds are together. Use a dry iron for this, you cannot use a muslin as you obscure the work. Use only the toe of the iron and take care not to allow it to touch the right side of the garment.

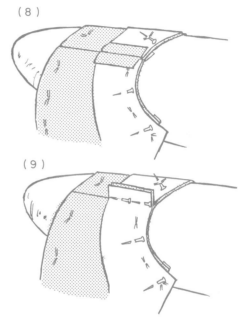

(8)

(9)

(iv)   With dress still on the sleeve board lift the facing edges and pin together so that the two creases meet (Fig. 9).

(v)   Remove dress from sleeve board and tack the two shoulder joins in the facing.

(vi)   Machine each join from neck outwards. Remove tackings and press open. Work on the sleeve board again and use only the toe of the dry iron at first. With a synthetic fabric press again with steam iron, but make sure the iron does not stray onto the garment and overpress or mark the shoulder area.

(vii)   Trim down the raw edges to 6mm ($\frac{1}{4}$in.) cutting corners off at an angle, to reduce bulk.

(viii)   Tack the entire facing to the neck, from centre back round to centre front, down front

(10)

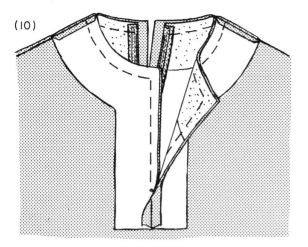

seam and the same on the second side (Fig. 10).

(ix)   Machine in place, working from the garment side in order to follow the marked neckline. Begin stitching at the centre front seam, lowering the needle into the work so that the first stitch starts only one stitch length away from the stitching at the centre front seam. This tiny gap will

(11a)

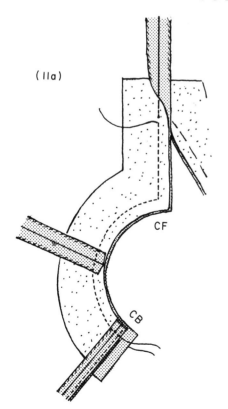

allow the facing to turn over without a wrinkle at that point.

Machine the right half of the neckline first as this is easier to position on the machine (Fig. 11a). With the left half you will have to cope with the bulk of the garment to the right of the needle. If your fabric is bulky this may be awkward, and if so, stitch for only 5cm (2in.) to ensure the machining lines up accurately, take work out of machine and, using tacking thread, run a row of accurate small tacks through the fitting line from the garment side, taking stitches right through to

(11b)

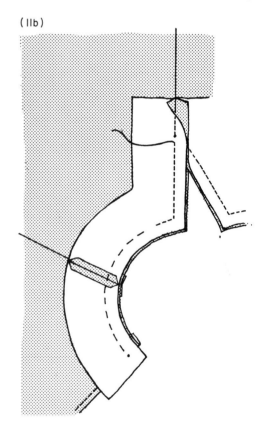

the facing. You can then turn it over and machine from the facing side, but using these tacks as a guide (Fig. 11b).

(x)   Remove all tacking stitches and tailor tacks. Fasten off firmly all ends of machining.

(xi)   Trim down the garment turning, with interfacing attached, to 6mm ($\frac{1}{4}$in.) wide, trim down the facing edge to 3mm ($\frac{1}{8}$in.) wide. If fabric frays badly, then leave them a little wider than this. The garment edge is left wider to avoid a ridge showing. Snip the turnings in towards the machine stitching every 6mm ($\frac{1}{4}$in.) all round curved section of neckline, including the shoulder seam area (Fig. 12). Use your small

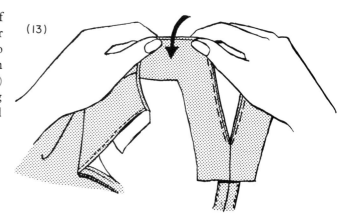

(13)

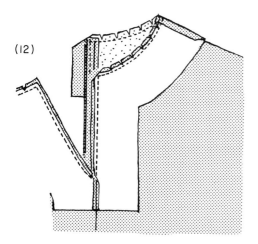

(12)

scissors and snip to just short of the line of stitching. Cut off the centre back and centre front corners.

(xii)   Place dress on sleeveboard, right side out, using a steam iron if possible; first press the stitching and then push the toe of the iron quickly round the neck under the facing, pushing it so that it stands up. Do not attempt to press the facing right over and don't keep the iron there too long.

(xiii)   Lift work off board and with wrong side towards you, roll the facing over towards you, working on only 1·3cm ($\frac{1}{2}$in.) at a time, holding it between thumb and forefinger and rolling until the join is right on the edge and there is no pleat in it. Roll the join 3mm ($\frac{1}{8}$in.) towards you so that it will not be seen in wear, and tack (Fig. 13). Use small stitches inserted one at a time, rolling each 1·3cm ($\frac{1}{2}$in.) before tacking. Tack just below the edge; the exact distance varies with the thickness of the fabric but it will be about 3mm ($\frac{1}{8}$in.) on thin materials, 6mm ($\frac{1}{4}$in.) on thicker ones. If you tack too close to the edge for the fabric it will

simply spring up, forcing the tacking stitches apart.

(xiv)   Press this edge from the wrong side. Press firmly with steam iron, or dry iron and damp muslin. Remember that short sharp movements will not leave tacking imprints on the edge, but heavy, prolonged pressing, especially with too cool an iron, will certainly leave marks.

(xv)   Trim the outer edge of the facing to level it off and neaten by whatever method has proved successful on the rest of the raw edges. Press the neatening, not with the facing resting on the garment, but lift it away.

(xvi)   To hold the facing in position cut 5cm (2in.) lengths of Wundaweb and slip at intervals between facing and garment (Fig. 14). Place dress

(14)

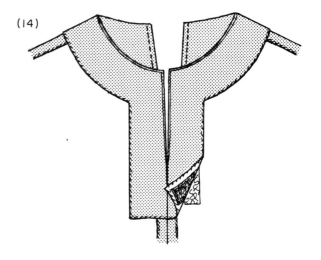

on sleeveboard first to keep it in shape. If the facing is very narrow in places the Wundaweb can be cut in half. If the fabric frays badly, or is springy, it will help if you first push very narrow pieces of Wundaweb right up close to the neck join and press to make it adhere, before putting in the larger pieces. Press first on the wrong side, on the facing itself using a steam iron, then press a little more firmly, but before it cools turn to the right side and press again, using a cloth if necessary to protect the fabric. This double pressing with steam will melt Wundaweb thoroughly and it will be held firmly in place. If ever the facing does lift away, simply re-press, slipping in another piece of Wundaweb if it seems necessary. Also, by turning quickly to the right side you can correct any wrinkles that may be forming, before the Wundaweb cools.

If your fabric is soft, it helps support the slit neckline of the basic dress to slip a longer piece of Wundaweb under that section of the neck.

3.4 Waist join

Any alterations made at fitting which changed the position of darts or seams should have been checked, so that they now all match up. Ends of seams and darts should all be cut away at an angle to reduce bulk.

(i)   Lay skirt out on table right side up, place bodice on it right side down. Match up fitting lines and match up darts, side seams and centre front seam. Check very carefully that centre back edges are equal in length each side from neck to waist and waist to hem.

(ii)   Place a pin across each seam join and tack with small stitches and an occasional back stitch. Tack up the centre back seam to the point where the zip will go.

(iii)   Remove pins and fit. If a belt is to be worn this should be put on. Mark any adjustments necessary where the seam is uneven or where it shows above or below the belt. If the exact posi-

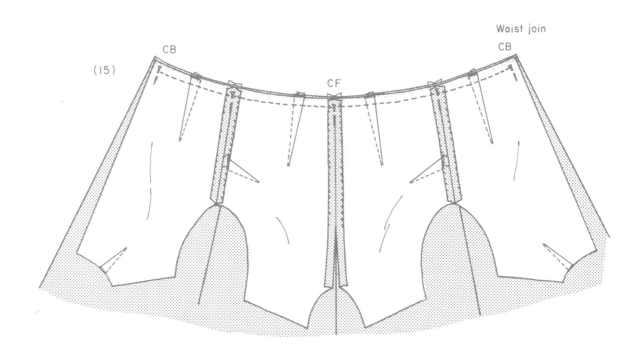

tion of the waist is difficult to find place the petersham fitting guide round as an indication.

(iv)   Remove dress and mark alterations. Re-tack and try on again.

(v)   Tack a length of tape or seam binding along the seam on the skirt side.

(vi)   Replace pins across seams and machine from the bodice side, going slowly over the pins (Fig. 16).

(vii)   Remove pins and tacking stitches. Trim the raw edges to 1·3cm (½in.). Press the join open and then on medium and lightweight fabrics press them both up into the bodice and neaten together by overcasting or zig-zag. (Fig. 17.) On heavier fabrics press join open, snip occasionally and neaten edges separately (Fig. 17b).

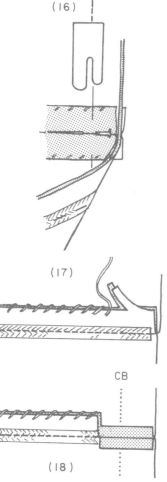

(viii)   At the centre back seam cut the turnings down to 6mm (¼in.) for 2·5cm (1in.) of the seam and press open, snipping the lower one if the waist join is pressed up (Fig. 18).

(ix)   Join and stitch the centre back seam, neaten edges right up the neck ready for inserting the zip (Fig. 19).

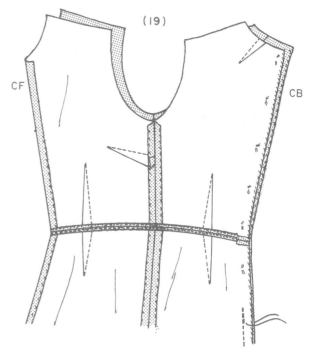

3.5 Zip fasteners

This is an efficient and professional looking fastening provided it is inserted with care and the following points noted. The zip can be inserted before or after the facings are attached.

General points

(i)   Zip fasteners are rarely faulty when you buy them, they are made by the mile on highly mechanized machinery and are thoroughly tested before leaving the factory. However, if you buy a cheap unlabelled zip it may be made from inferior materials.

(ii)   Your zip may break if the garment is too tight or if the zip is really too short and you are straining the end stop every time you wear it.

(iii)   Stitching across the bottom does not strengthen it, (the end of the seam, and the end stop take the strain between them) and it may cause a bulge especially on thick fabrics.

(iv)   Fasten off all threads firmly.

(v)   Do not stretch the fabric either when tacking or pressing. Remember that the zip tape is rigid and cannot stretch but your fabric is soft and often on the bias.

(vi)   Always stitch from the bottom of the zip up to the open end and then any push on the fabric will not result in a bulge at the bottom. Where you have to put a zip into an edge that is already finished at the top it is obviously essential that there is no movement at all. In this case anchor the top edges firmly, with plenty of over-sewing, before tacking and then put the zip in by hand, even if you then machine afterwards on top of your hand sewing.

(vii)   The decision to stitch in a zip by hand or machine should depend on the fabric you are using. The zip tape is a strong, heavy cotton or synthetic twill and if your fabric is different in weight and texture when folded double, e.g. chiffon, silk, velvet, and many lightweight fabrics, sew by hand because the chances are that the pressure of the machine foot will push the top fabric but not the heavier tape beneath. Also, with a very bulky fabric such as tweed, or some Crimplene, the pressure of the machine stitching can cause a bulky ridge. You may be deliberately trying to create this effect but if not, sew the zip in by hand.

(viii)   Modern reputable zip fasteners do not slide undone, but on a tight fitting garment it helps to lessen the strain if you put a fastening at the top – a hook and bar or a tiny strip of Velcro. This should be fastened up before the zip is closed. If there is a collar, waistband etc., then this serves the same purpose and other fastening is unnecessary. The hook should never be used to fill a gap at the top.

(ix)   Choose your zip according to your fabric, putting the finer zips into lightweight fabrics and metal ones into heavy fabrics. Also, the character of the garment should be considered. A metal zip is more in keeping with casual denim clothes, even a soft lightweight jersey denim. Invisible zips, where there is no stitching showing on the right side of the garment are excellent for skirts, trousers etc.

(x)   Where the length of the opening is critical for getting into the garment, calculate what length zip will be required. For example, only very slim women can step into a skirt with an 20cm (8in.) zip and no waistband. If a waistband is added, it lowers the zip by 7cm (3in.) or so and makes the total opening that much longer.

Measure the widest part that the garment has to go over; this may be thighs, hips, shoulders or bust. Cut a piece of tape or long piece of spare fabric, pin up this measurement and put it on to try it. Lengthen it if you find you cannot get it on then check that the total length of opening on the garment, e.g. waist plus two sides of zip, or neckline plus two sides of zip, at least equals this measurement. If you have 5cm (2in.) of ease as well, then so much the better.

Even edges insertion

This is probably the easiest method of inserting a zip for anyone not very experienced and it is simpler to do on a plain neckline that is finished with a facing. Otherwise you have the problem of coping with the top of the zip.

Method 1

(i)   Turn in and tack both edges of the centre back seam so that the tailor tacks are on the folded edge. Press these edges by placing the work on the sleeve board right side down, anchor the two neck points with pins and place another just below the bottom of the opening, plunging the pins into the sleeve board padding. This will help to ensure that both edges remain the same length and do not stretch. Press carefully with steam iron, or dry iron and damp muslin (Fig. 20).

If the garment is mounted the under fabric acts as support for the zip, but if using a single layer of very lightweight material try slipping a narrow length of Wundaweb in as you tack the edges ready for pressing.

(ii)   Remove work from board. With zip closed and starting at the neck edge place fold of fabric a little more than half way across the teeth. Tack. The effect of making a tacking stitch is to draw the edge back off the teeth a little, this is why it is best to start with it well over the teeth (Fig. 21). Tack the second side, again starting from the neck to ensure that the slider is positioned just below the fitting line, and to make sure the fitting lines are level.

(iii) Overcast the two folded edges together, using tacking thread (Fig. 22).

(iv) Sew in the zip. Whether sewing with a hand prick stitch or by machine, start at the bottom and work up to the neck edge. This avoids the possibility of a bubble at the bottom. In addition, if you can resist the temptation to stitch across the bottom, this too avoids a bubble. Do not try to stitch too close to the teeth as this drags the material off the zip and it will show as soon as you open it. If sewing by machine, do not use too small a stitch (Fig. 23).

(v) Undo the tacking but not the oversewing and press the stitching flat on both sides of the garment. Finally unpick the oversewing and run the zip gently up and down a few times.

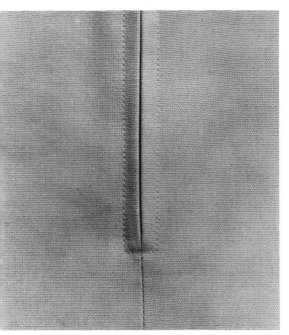

11   Zip inserted by even hems methods (courtesy Lightning Fasteners Ltd)

(20)   (21)

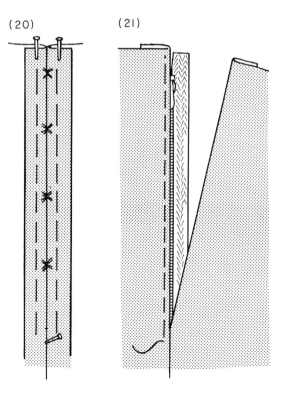

(22)   (23)

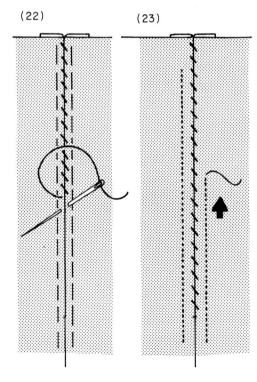

Uneven edge insertion

Some people prefer this method wherever they insert a conventionally toothed zip, and if there is to be a collar or a waistband added afterwards there is no problem.

The main advantage of this method is that the teeth are completely covered. To do this the zip must be tucked a little further under the flap part. There is no point whatever in doing it the way that is found on many bought clothes, simply a narrow turning on one side, a wider one on the other, a continuous row of machining right round and a zip that still shows.

(i)   Measure length of line of teeth against garment from fitting line. Place slider 3mm ($\frac{1}{8}$in.) below this line to allow for fabric turning over later. Close the seam to just above the bottom stop, press open but do not neaten raw edges yet.

(ii)   Turn back, tack and press the turning on the side that is to be the wider side or covering flap (Fig. 24).

(iii)   Arrange opening so that the piece just tacked is folded over out of the way, wrong side towards you, so leaving the underneath turning right side up. Place zip, closed, in position, face down, with the teeth exactly over the seam line marked by tailor tacks. Tack close to the teeth taking an occasional back stitch to hold it in place (Fig. 25).

(iv)   Put zip or piping foot on machine, adjust and machine close to the teeth, working from the zip side, starting at the bottom and stitching from end to end of the tape (Fig. 25).

Remove tacks. Fasten off machine ends. Turn zip over, fold turning under and tack through the two layers of fabric and the zip tape (Fig. 26).

(24)

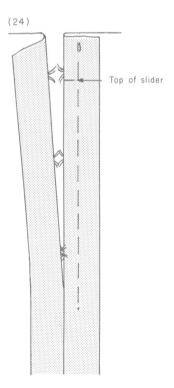

Top of slider

(25)

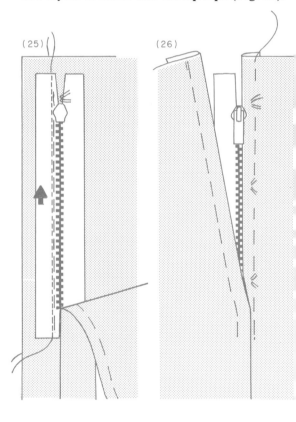

(26)

(v)   Press this edge now as you will not be able to reach it comfortably later. Arrange the zip on the sleeve board so that the fabric will not stretch. Drape your damp muslin cloth over the toe of the iron, holding the cloth up with the other hand

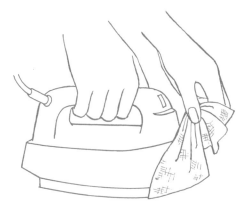

Press by placing the iron toe close against the teeth, moving it along after you have examined the pressing. Do not press over the teeth or the muslin will be above the part to be pressed rather than on it and the effect is to create steam between muslin and garment which, without the iron to smooth it out, will cause bubbling.

(vi)   Bring the previously tacked folded edge over to cover the zip, matching the fold to the tailor tacks beside the zip. Anchor the top level

with one pin, then, starting from the bottom tack beside the teeth to hold the flap side down. Oversew the fold to the garment (Fig. 27). If your fabric is slippery, or if your zip is a particularly heavy one, it helps to oversew the folded edge in position first, and then tack beside the teeth.

(vii)   Stitch by hand or machine. Stitch from the right side, starting at the bottom and working up to the raw edges of the garment (Fig. 28). 1·3cm ($\frac{1}{2}$in.) from the slider, slope your stitching out at an angle. This makes a wider pocket to conceal the slider.

Remove all tacking. Press the row of stitching, not the zip itself, with the toe of the iron and muslin cloth, as before.

Concealed zips

Totally concealed zips such as the one made by Lightning Ltd are different from conventional zips because when fastened, the teeth are on the back of the zip and therefore cannot show. This means that having stitched close to the teeth, the fabric comes together, looking just like a seam. These zips are slightly different to insert but very easy because even a beginner doesn't have to

12   A concealed zip – looks like a seam (courtesy Lightning Fasteners Ltd)

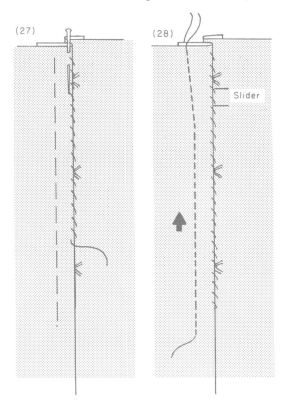

(27)

(28)

Slider

worry about whether the stitching is straight. Use a 23cm (9in.) zip unless hips are very slim, in which case use a 20cm (8in.) one, 55cm (22in.) for a dress.

(i)   Open the zip and place it beside the seam where it is to go. Put the top stop 6mm ($\frac{1}{4}$in.) below the fitting line and at the bottom mark off with chalk a point level with the top of the zip slider (Fig. 29).

(ii)   Close up the seam where the zip is to go, using a big machine stitch. Sew from the end of the seam already sewn to the outer edge of the garment to avoid a pucker at the bottom (Fig. 30).

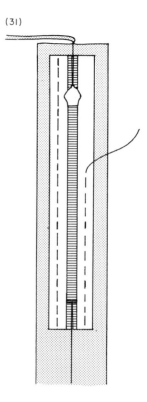

(31)

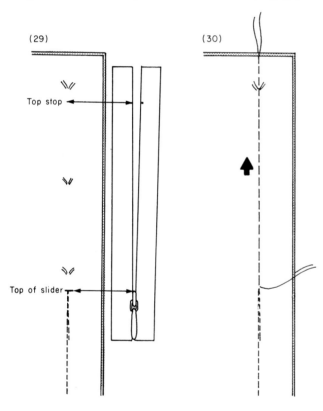

(29)

(30)

Top stop

Top of slider

(iii)   Press this seam open. Neaten the raw edges if they have not already been done when the rest of the seam was neatened.

(iv)   Place the zip on the back of the seam right side down, lining up the centre of the zip with the seam line. Tack, taking the stitches through the tape and through the turning but not through the garment as with an ordinary zip. Tack firmly

with a back stitch every couple of inches (Fig. 31).

(v)   Pull out the machine stitches holding the seam together. Open the zip. To sew in the zip, stitch as close as possible to the teeth, rolling them over to get really close (Fig. 32). Begin stitching at the top of each side. Sew each side through the turnings only.

How to stitch:

(a) By hand

Wax the thread for strength and back stitch from end to end of the tape; beginning from the top of the zip work as close as possible to the slider, moving it a little if it helps, although the stitching will be a little further away at this point. If you are worried that hand sewing may not be strong enough, work a row of machining 6mm ($\frac{1}{4}$in.) away through tape and turning (Fig. 32).

(b) By machine

(32)

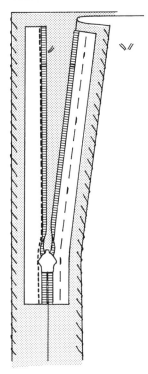

An ordinary piping or zip foot can be used, guiding the work to keep the needle close to the zip.

Stitch until reaching the slider and then stop and remove the work. Stitch the other side. Move the slider and complete by stitching from the previous stitching down to the end of the tape. This stitching will have to be further from the teeth but if you left a gap shorter than the zip length as explained under point 1 at the beginning, it will not show.

You may find it easier to do the last part by hand, threading the ends of machining into a needle and back stitching.

(vi)   Fasten off all ends and cut off close. Open and close the zip a few times gently to roll the teeth back into position.

3.6 Setting in sleeves

Establish a well-fitting armhole on the dress before setting in the sleeve. The difficulty lies in putting together the two very different curves of armhole and sleeve but at the same time allowing sufficient ease for movement and achieving a good hang. The temptation to solve the problem of ease by inserting a gathering thread should be resisted in a plain-topped sleeve as this can only result in a gathered sleeve.

The setting in is best tackled in two stages, the underarm, followed by the sleeve head, and if you first appreciate the way in which you are trying to distribute the ease you will find it easier. No ease at all is required at the underarm section, but the sleeve must on no account be stretched. Of the remaining fullness at the sleeve head arrange a little for the two inches above the underarm section; more than half of what is left should go to the front between shoulder seam and balance mark while less than half is used at the back because the shoulder is more shallow and there is no protruberance of arm bone as there is at the front.

Tacking in sleeves
(i)   Turn bodice right side out and have sleeves right side out.
(ii)   Pick up the right sleeve ready to set into the right armhole. Check that you have the correct sleeve by folding it along the seam and smoothing out the head. The raw edges will not be level because the front has been hollowed out and the back extended to allow for movement (Fig. 33).
(iii)   Place sleeve seam to underarm seam and pin (Fig. 34). Place together the stitching lines of the underarm for about 7·5cm (3in.) on either side of that first pin. Tack with fairly small stitches. Fasten off tacking and remove pins.
(iv)   Tack in the underarm section of the left sleeve immediately in the same way.
(v)   To set in the sleeve head, turn the bodice inside out and roll back the top section of the armhole. Pull the top part of the sleeve through and lay it in position on the bodice with fitting lines matching. Slip your fingers under the two

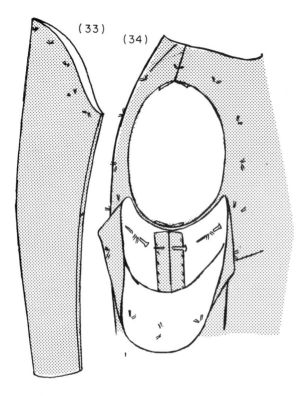

(33)

(34)

turnings to support them while you pin. Place a pin in the sleeve at right angles to the raw edges. Continue to pin at intervals, dispersing the fullness with each pin you insert. Don't allow a fold of fabric to develop between any two pins. If it does, remove a few pins and spread the ease again (Fig. 35). The raw edges will flute as you pin, but at the fitting line itself there should be no folds of fabric. As you pin remember the

positions described earlier where more and less fullness is required.

Move to the second sleeve immediately and pin to ensure that they both look the same.

(vi)   Tack the sleeve head with very small stitches, removing each pin as you reach it.

If, occasionally, with some twill weave synthetics you find it impossible to ease in the sleeve in this way, you can run a row of regular machine stitching round the sleeve head on the fitting line. This must not be pulled up but it will help to prevent the sleeve stretching and becoming longer.

Sewing in sleeves
After fitting and adjusting, the sleeves can be sewn in.

(i) By hand
On any soft, fairly thick, material or one with a surface interest, sew the sleeves in by hand. This ensures that the ease will not flatten into pleats as it sometimes does if you machine round the armhole.

If you hold the work with the sleeve uppermost as you did for tacking you will be able to control the ease as you stitch and make sure that you do not form any pleats or tucks in the sleeve head. However, stitching with the bodice towards you ensures a smoother line to the armhole. You may like to compromise by sewing from the armhole side for most of it (Fig. 36a) but turning it over when you start on the sleeve head section (Fig. 36b).

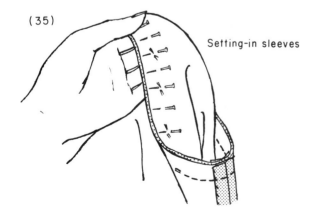

(35)

Setting-in sleeves

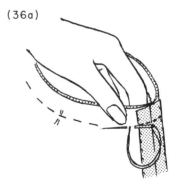

(36a)

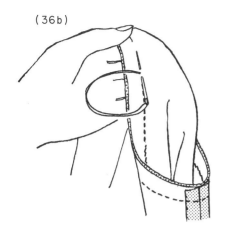

(36b)

Use double thread run through Beeswax to strengthen and bind it together and back stitch round the armhole close by your tackings. Take the needle half-way back each time, not right back to the previous stitch (Fig. 36c). This makes a much closer stitch. Pull the thread fairly tight although one of the advantages of hand sewing is that the tension is looser than that of machining and it means with sleeves that you will retain a soft, unpinched line.

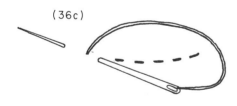

(36c)

(ii) By machine

If you are using cotton or any smooth thin material that would pull apart to reveal hand sewing, sew the sleeves in by machine. If you have a free arm on your machine, use it. Slip the armhole onto the arm with the sleeve uppermost so that you can watch the ease. Set the machine to a slightly smaller stitch than for seams and stitch slowly, working only two or three stitches at a time before easing the work round. On jersey fabric use a slight zig-zag stitch. Fasten off strongly by overlapping the machine stitching for at least 2·5cm (1in.).

(iii) Combining hand and machine stitching

If the fabric is thin and firm but you are worried about coping with the ease when it goes under the machine, back stitch the sleeve head only to anchor the difficult section and then machine round the whole armhole, stitching exactly on top of your hand sewing.

Trimming and neatening the armhole

On all except sheer fabrics trim off only the fraying edge of the turnings, leaving 1·3cm ($\frac{1}{2}$in.) to be neatened. This wide turning will support the head of the sleeve and keep it a good shape (Fig. 37a). Neaten the raw edges according to the

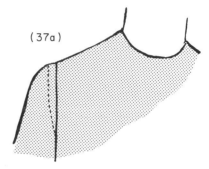

(37a)

fabric, using whatever method you have found best on the seams.

On transparent fabrics trim the edges to less than 1·3cm ($\frac{1}{2}$in.) and either overcast very neatly or turn the raw edges in towards each other and slip stitch together (Fig. 37b). The raw edges can be bound provided this doesn't add unsightly bulk (Fig. 37c).

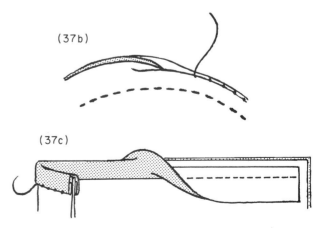

(37b)

(37c)

Pressing sleeves

The main part of the sleeve has been pressed during making up, but if it needs touching up slide a folded towel into the sleeve and press, turning it over to press underneath.

Press the sleeve head turnings into the sleeve but leave the underarm turnings unpressed and standing up inside the armhole.

To press the sleeve head, fold a towel into a cube and push it into the shoulder and just a little way into the sleeve head. Hold the towel in one hand with the garment over it and with the other hand just drape a damp muslin over it and then press with the toe of the iron, working only along the sleeve seam (Fig. 38). Press in this way up the front armhole, over the top and down the back, but not under the arm. Change to the other sleeve without putting the garment down, press the second sleeve and put the garment immediately on a hanger.

On soft fabrics such as wool, remove the cloth quickly after pressing and gently pinch up the top of the sleeve to shape it, taking hold of the sleeve, the turnings inside and part of the shoulder seam. When working on cottons and some rayons you may be able to use a steam iron to press.

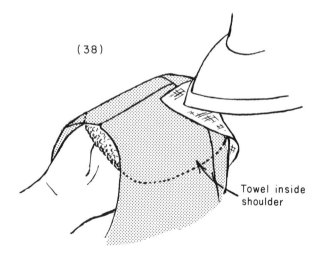

(38)

Towel inside shoulder

3.7 Buttonholes

Piped buttonholes

These are the easiest buttonholes to do apart from machine-made ones and the method is the same as for making a piped or jetted pocket.

(i) Position

In wear the button sits at the end of the button-hole so the distance between the edge of the fabric and the start of the buttonhole must equal the diameter of the button, otherwise, when fastened the button will hang over the edge. If the edge is shaped, as in the case of the tab, it goes further back still if it is a big button.

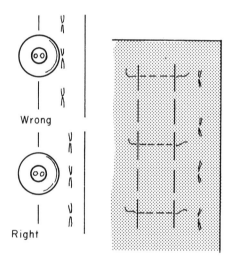

Wrong

Right

(ii) Marking

Mark the position of the buttonhole with chalk or tacking, putting one line to indicate the start of the buttonhole and another to show the end of it. Mark across between the lines to show the horizontal position of the buttonhole.

(iii) Preparation of piping

Cut a strip of fabric on the straight grain 2·5cm (1in.) wide, and long enough to make strips for each side of each buttonhole plus turnings at each end. Iron Bondaweb (paper-backed adhesive) to wrong side. Tear off the paper when cool. Fold strip in half down the middle and press to melt the adhesive and so stick the strip.

Trim the piping down as narrow as you can for the fabric. The width will be about 7mm ($\frac{1}{4}$in.) for fine fabrics but wider on thicker fabrics. The finished piping will be half the width you cut it.

(iv) Attaching pipings

Cut pipings into equal lengths and place with cut edges meeting over the buttonhole mark. Tack. (Fig 39a.) Re-mark the exact length of the button-hole with chalk, across the pipings.

Machine each piping (Fig. 39b). Use a small stitch, start in the middle and work to one end, turn, stitch to far end, turn and stitch back to the middle. This gives you extra strength but it also means that you don't have to sew in all the ends of thread to fasten them off. Remove tackings.

On wrong side cut the centre of the buttonhole between the rows of stitching and then cut out to the corners (Fig. 39c).

Push pipings through to wrong side. On right side oversew folded edges together and press (Fig. 39d).

Tuck end triangles back into position and hold in place by working a stab stitch through all layers across the end of the buttonhole (Fig. 39e).

Fold facing or backing fabric into position at the back of the buttonhole and tack. Mark the exact size of the buttonhole with pins and cut between. Turn in the raw edge and quickly hem round to finish (Fig. 39f).

Hand-worked buttonholes

These need skill and patience and should only be attempted on a garment after a lot of practice.

Mark positions as for piped buttonholes.

(i) Thread

On fine fabrics use your machine thread, on thicker ones use buttonhole twist or special thick

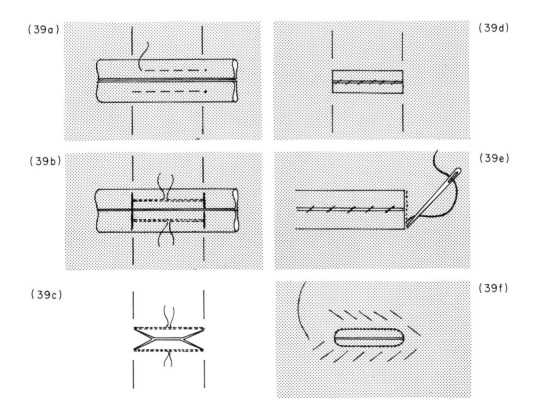

(39a) (39b) (39c) (39d) (39e) (39f)

thread such as Coats' Bold Stitch Drima. Use a
long single piece with a knot.

(ii) Cutting

Only cut as you work each one. Push a pin
through one end of the marked buttonhole and
out at the other; fold flat and snip the fabric.
Remove pin and snip carefully into the holes left
by the pin.

(iii) Stitching

Begin at the end furthest from the edge of the
fabric, pulling the thread up between the layers
but leaving the knot on the wrong side a little
way off, to be cut off later (Fig. 40a). Work button-

Handmade

(40a)

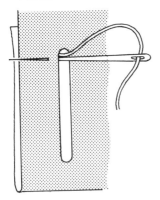

hole stitch towards you taking short stitches and
winding the thread round the needle towards
you. Pull the thread again after making the stitch
to settle the knot in position. The knots should
touch so there should be spaces between the
uprights.

At the button end make the stitches even
shorter and pull the knobs on to the top of the
fabric to allow room for the button shanks. Work
an odd number of stitches, say 5, round the end
(Fig. 40b).

At the far end take one stitch through the first
stitch worked to close up the end, then work a
small short bar of stitches across the end. These
stitches should embed in the fabric and hardly

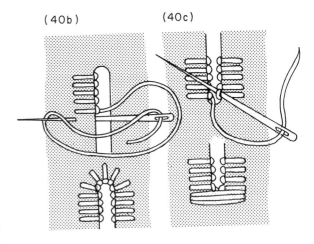

(40b)   (40c)

show (Fig. 40c). Some people work a big bar of
buttonhole stitches here but they show badly
even when the button is fastened and look ugly.

Tailor's buttonhole

A gimp thread is inserted into the edge of the
buttonhole for strength and the stitches worked
over it. Use tailor's gimp or several strands of
thread, or a piece of buttonhole twist.

You hold the gimp under your thumb as you
work so the buttonhole stitches have to be worked
in the other direction, i.e. away from you. You
therefore wind the thread the other way round the
needle, i.e. away from you.

After completion pull the gimp tight and pass
both ends through to wrong side. Cut off the ends
and hold down with several oversewing stitches.

3.8 Buttons and press studs

Buttons

Buttons must be sewn on through two layers of
fabric and one layer of interfacing at least, otherwise the strain on the fabric will tear it in a short
time. If these three layers are not available then
extra must be added. This can be a piece of firm
fabric such as poplin or lawn, or, for a single
button, a square of tape, folded, or a piece of
canvas or Vilene. The choice of reinforcement
depends on the garment and the position of the

buttons. Also, if a fabric is being used that obviously will not be strong enough even as a double layer, e.g. chiffon, mohair, then yet another layer of something much firmer must be added and if this would spoil the outward appearance, the obviously a buttoned fastening is the wrong choice anyway.

Choice of needle and thread

Use a larger between needle than you have for the rest of the hand sewing on the garment; this is to make a bigger hole to take the thread.

For coats and heavy garments use button thread, usually made of linen, for lighter fabrics use sewing thread. Thread the needle, pull the thread through double and knot the end. Run this through beeswax from knot to needle three times, then twist the thread between your palms, starting from the knot. Twist one palm-length at a time. Wind the twisted section round your thumb and this places the next section ready for twisting. This covering of wax makes it stronger and the twisting also makes it stronger and in addition prevents the threads from parting as you sew (Fig. 41).

It is a good idea to thread several button needles, say one for every two buttons before you

begin. You are then not tempted to make do with less thread at the end of a needle.

Pin up the garment opening with pins between the buttonholes. Insert the button needle right in the far end of the buttonhole on the centre front line or wherever your mark is (Fig. 42). Take needle through to wrong side, unpin

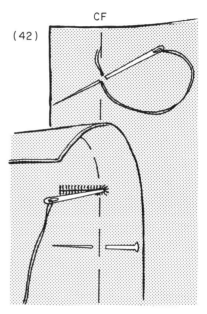

and take off the buttonhole side. Bring needle up to right side. Make one more stitch like this through to wrong side and back to right. Take one stitch through the fabric from right side only without stabbing, cut off knot.

You are now ready to sew on the button. Take at least 6 stitches through the button, working the stitches from the right side, going into the button, into the fabric, and out of the fabric in one movement. (Fig. 43.) The advantage of this method as opposed to stabbing through to the wrong side is that it gives a neater wrong side and also you have to keep the button on its side and it is easier to make a shank. Keep the button lifted sufficiently off the garment to allow for the thickness of the buttonhole side. The shank must be at least 6mm ($\frac{1}{4}$in.) long on thick fabrics and never shorter than 3mm ($\frac{1}{8}$in.) on anything. As you

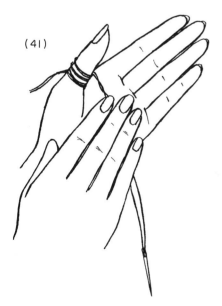

take the stitches, keep lifting it to check the distance. It is not a good idea to use a match or something similar because this will only produce a very short shank and you will in addition have to use stabbing stitches which will make the wrong side look untidy. If the button has a shank it is unlikely to be quite long enough so add a little more when you sew on.

Try as far as possible to keep your stitches roughly in the same place. If the button has two holes they should lie parallel with the buttonhole (Fig. 43), if there are four holes they should + not ×.

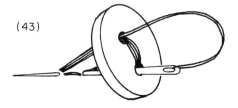

(43)

After working plenty of stitches through the button, bring the needle out close to the shank and wind the thread round. Start at the base and wind three or four times, give the thread a tug to tighten it, then wind again from button down to base, pull tight (Fig. 44).

Insert needle and take two or three stitches through the base of the shank (Fig. 45a). Take needle through to wrong side, tidy up the back by working a few loop stitches to draw the threads together. Fasten off (Fig. 45b).

The button should now be standing clear of the garment. On coating, leather, suede, etc., it will

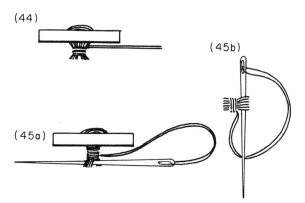

(44)

(45b)

(45a)

save possible tearing to choose four-hole buttons and sew small backing buttons on the back, taking the needle right through both each time, but making a shank only on the top.

Press studs

Choose a small size, e.g. 00, as there will be no strain at this point.

The knob section is less bulky and therefore goes on the outer part of the garment. Slip a pin through the hole in the centre and pin it in the correct position just a little inside the corner (Fig. 46a). Use single thread run through wax,

Attaching dress studs

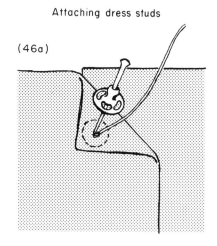

(46a)

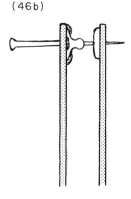

(46b)

start with a knot and make two stitches right under the press stud, where the pin is. Slide the press stud down the pin to the fabric, take one stitch through each hole to hold the press stud in position so that it will not move. Remove pin. Attach press stud by working buttonhole stitch closely in each hole. You will be able to work about four stitches in each hole. Fasten off firmly just beside the press stud.

Fasten up the buttons.

Slip a pin through from the right side of the garment, through the hole in the press stud and then through the hole in the other half of the press stud – the well (Fig. 46b). Close up the two layers of fabric and pierce the under side with the pin. Lift top layer a little and work a back stitch exactly where the pin is. Remove pin, slide well section on to it and anchor it in position over the stitch.

Work one stitch in each hole, remove pin and attach with close buttonhole stitch as before.

3.9 Hems

If a hemline shows, it is not usually because the stitches show, but it is more likely to be due to excess bulk of fabric either within the hem or because the hem is too deep, or bad pressing.

The stitches disturb the back of the fabric slightly so it is essential to leave the thread fairly loose otherwise after some wear the weight of the hem pulling on a tight thread will cause a mark to appear. The danger of marking is reduced if the garment is mounted. The turned up raw edge must be neatened in the least bulky way possible for the fabric while still preventing fraying. Usually, the method used for neatening seams will be found satisfactory.

Some fabrics and garments can be treated differently, e.g. where there is a lining, but the following method is best for dress hem, sleeve hems and trouser hems.

Preparation

(i)   Having marked the length at fitting probably with a row of pins, check carefully that pairs of seams are equal in length, e.g. side seams, sleeve seams, inside trouser leg seams. If there is a known figure fault such as one protruding hip then this obviously cannot be done. Do not com-

pare the centre front seam with the centre back.

(ii)   Adjust any pins that appear to be out of line. If the fabric is particularly slippery or if you know that more fittings are still to be done, run a row of tacking round on the pins so that they can be removed before they fall out.

(iii)   At the seams trim away the turning to 6mm ($\frac{1}{4}$in.) from the edge to just past the hemline (Fig. 47).

If the seam is angled, as it is for instance on a sleeve, it will also help to snip the turning at the hemline (Fig. 48).

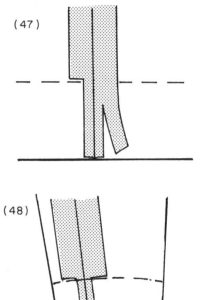

(47)

(48)

(iv)   Turn up the surplus fabric and tack with small stitches just inside the folded edge (Fig. 49a). This distance varies with the fabric being used; on thin lightweight material the tacking should be no more than 3mm ($\frac{1}{8}$in.) down, whereas on a bulky fabric you will find it springs up and parts the tackings if it is not at least 6mm ($\frac{1}{4}$in.) down.

(v)   When turning up a skirt hem lay the work on the table right side out and centre front on top and hem towards you. Fold back the top part of

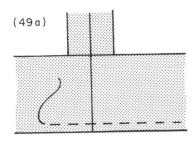

(49a)

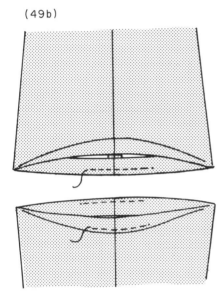

(49b)

the skirt and begin by tacking the 20cm (8in.) section immediately in front of you, keeping the work on the table. Swivel the skirt round and arrange it so that you now tack 20cm (8in.) or so at the centre front. Move it again and tack the side seam section, then the other (Fig. 49b). Finally fill in any areas not tacked. This method avoids dragging and ensures any surplus due to flare in the skirt is evenly distributed.

(vi)   Press the fold. Use the sleeve board and make sure the hem is not being stretched. Arrange part of it on the sleeve board lengthways, placing it in a curve if that is the shape of the garment. Press on the wrong side only by whatever method is being used for that fabric. Press once only; the final pressing is done later.

Sleeves and trousers should be turned inside out so that you can slide them onto the sleeve board to press.

Press only the fold of the fabric, using the toe and side of the iron, never let the iron rest on the raw edge of the fabric.

(vii)   When cool, run a row of fairly large tacking stitches round the hem to hold the surplus fabric up and try the garment on. If you are going to wear a belt on the dress this must be put on.

If any parts are not right, mark that section with pins. Make any alterations by undoing the tacking not only at that point but for a good way on either side, press out the crease with medium hot iron and damp muslin, and turn up again to give a better line. If the length is totally wrong all round, mark the correct length with one pin before pulling out all tacking, pressing out the crease, and starting again.

When satisfied with the hemline, remove the second row of tacking holding the raw edge.

Depth of hem
This depends mainly on the amount of shape in the hem but also on the fabric. A skirt hem tends to be as deep as possible in order to weight the garment so that it hangs well but if this causes problems with surplus fabric due to flare then it should be made narrower. Where seams are shaped, as on sleeves and trousers, the hem should not be too deep.

If the fabric is very light weight a deep hem helps it to hang well but if it is also transparent it may be better to make a very narrow hem for the sake of appearance.

The following is a guide for most medium weight fabrics:

Dress or skirt hem 5cm (2in.)
Sleeve 2cm ($\frac{3}{4}$in.)
Trouser 2·5–4cm (1–1$\frac{1}{2}$in.)

Use gauge or marker and measure evenly round, marking with chalk (Fig. 50a). Trim surplus fabric away, using medium scissors. Neaten the raw edge, preferably by overcasting as it is softer, but you can zig-zag by machine, especially on trouser and sleeve hems, if you wish.

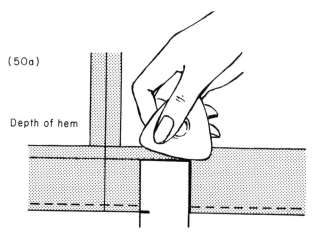

(50a)

Depth of hem

Press this neatening, but not against the garment.

Tack hem flat, stitching a little below the neatening.

Stitching

Use short pieces of thread and, holding the work with the fold towards you, lift the raw edge and catch stitch just underneath. Take only one thread on the garment and then a small amount of the hem. Stitches should be about 6mm ($\frac{1}{4}$in.) apart. Keep the thread fairly loose, in fact on a jersey fabric it is a good idea deliberately to leave a little loop every few centimetres. The catch stitch should not be too far under this edge otherwise you will be likely to catch it at some time and tear the stitching (Fig. 50b).

In place of stitching you could use Wundaweb, especially on trousers and sleeves, but try it out first, in case it provides too much stiffness in some fabrics. The hem should be finished at a depth of

(50b)

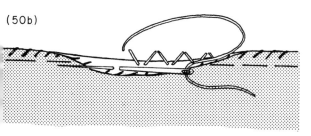

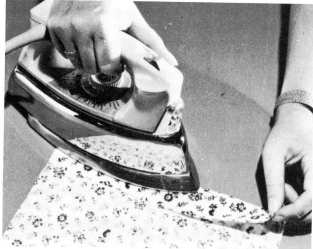

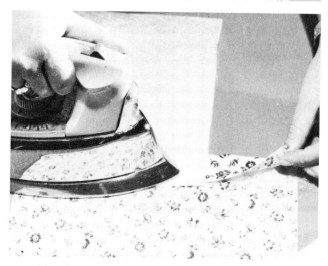

13 Turning up a hem with Wundaweb *(courtesy Vilene Ltd)*

4cm ($1\frac{1}{2}$in.) for Wundaweb, neatening the edge as before. Fold down the hem, place Wundaweb in position, cutting and overlapping it to make it curve (Fig. 50c). Flap hem up again so that it covers the Wundaweb and press with medium-hot iron and damp cloth. Do not press over the hem edge.

Finishing

Remove all tacking stitches. Press the hem up to, but not over, the edge. If you feel this is not

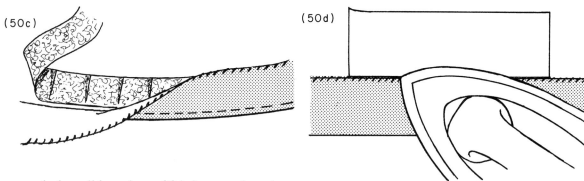

(50c)

(50d)

enough then slide a piece of fabric up against the edge to bring it all up to the same level and press lightly over the area, not allowing the weight of the iron too firmly on the work (Fig. 50d). Turn garment to right side and press lightly.

SECTION 3

ADAPTATIONS

Pinafore dress

Description
Simple V-neck pinafore dress with bold top stitching and tab. Zip is in centre back but it could be set into the centre front seam in which case the tab would have to be made to fasten either with buttonholes or Velcro.

Tab and imitation jetted pocket can be self fabric, contrast or suede or leather.

Fabric suggestion
Donegal type wool or mixture, small check design or any plain firm cloth.

Pressing
Hot iron on damp muslin, plenty of pressure. Use pressing block on seams etc. and allow to cool before moving.

Haberdashery
30cm (½yd) Vilene, Firm Iron-on 56cm (22in.) zip for back or 40cm (16in.) if inserted at front, 2·5cm (1in.) 2 buttons, 4cm (1½in.) Velcro, 2 reels Drima, 1 reel Bold-stitch Drima, Wunda-web, small piece of Bondaweb, small piece of lining fabric.

Figure types
This will suit most people but the short tab will especially flatter a thick waist as it breaks up the waist-line. A pinafore dress is always good on the broad shouldered figure. For a simpler effect omit the pocket and the tab belt.

Basic Pinafore dress. Piped top pocket,
Waist tab,
Back zip or can have front zip in CF seam

Order of making up

(i)   Make imitation pocket after establishing position at first fitting.

(ii)   Follow order for making basic dress except that you attach armhole facings instead of setting in sleeves.

(iii)   Make and attach tab after establishing the exact length needed to fall between the darts.

Fitting points

Tack up bodice and try on over blouse or jumper, let out side seams if necessary and see whether the armhole needs lowering further.

V-neck and facings

Preparation

(i)   The pattern

Use basic bodice and skirt pieces. Measure 15·2cm (6in.) down centre front. Rule a line from there to the shoulder. Mark pocket position 7·5cm (3in.) long halfway between shoulder and underarm. Lower the armhole 13mm ($\frac{1}{2}$in.) on back and front (Fig. 1). Trace neck facings to the new neckline, marking in 1·5cm ($\frac{5}{8}$in.) for seam allowance and then 5·5cm (2in.) for facing width (Fig. 2).

Pattern   (1)

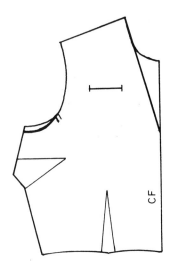
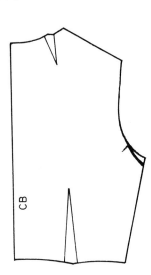

Neck facing   (2)

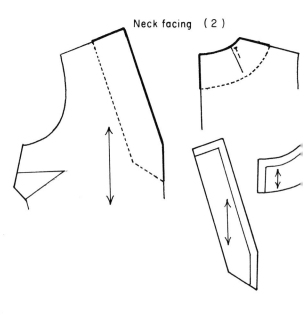

Preparing armhole facings

(a) The pattern: pin back and front bodice to paper, overlapping the shoulder turnings. Trace the armhole edge and about 5cm (2in.) of side seam. Remove pattern and mark in facing. First measure 1·5cm ($\frac{5}{8}$in.) for seam allowance then 5cm (2in.) for facing width, allowing 6mm ($\frac{1}{4}$in.) for neatening at outer edge. Straight grain should run in the same direction as on bodice front (Fig. 3).

(b) Cutting Out: do not cut facings until after first fitting in case alterations are made. Then lay pattern on double fabric with straight grain correct. Cut out.

(c) Interfacing: armholes are not usually interfaced although the top few inches of the armhole is often included with the shoulder. This gives support and is better on a sleeveless garment (Fig. 4). With this style there is also a pocket so it is necessary to interface that area as well, either by placing a small piece of interfacing under the pocket position, or by cutting the interfacing to include it, taking the line about 2·5cm (1in.) below the pocket and across to the armhole.

(ii) Cutting Out

Cut neckline higher until after the first fitting. Do not cut neck facings until any neckline adjustments have been made.

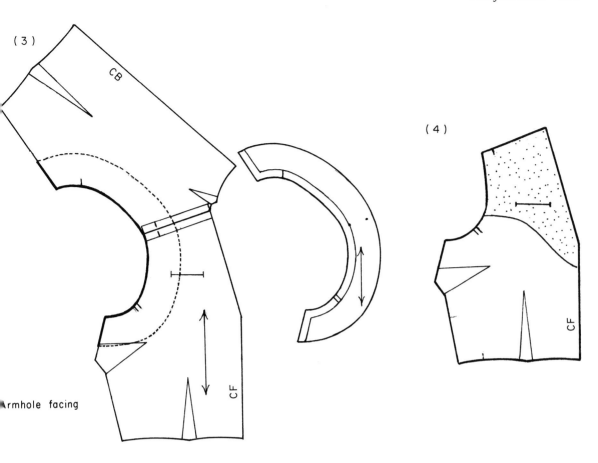

(3)

CB

Armhole facing

CF

(4)

CF

(iii) Interfacing

Interface the whole of the neck and shoulders as this gives more support to a sleeveless garment.

Lay bodice front onto a double layer of Vilene and cut out neck, shoulder and armhole to 2·5cm (1in.) below the pocket position. Remove bodice and cut interfacing in a curve across to centre front.

Press into position wrong side.

Facing V-Neck

After the garment has been interfaced and stitched the neckline should not stretch but before this you are likely to stretch it every time you lift it up. To avoid this handle it as follows:

(i) Cut out bodice, tailor tack, cut interfacing and press into position. Do as much of this as you can without lifting the pieces of bodice and when you move them to the iron, lift the whole piece, do not let the neckline take any weight.

(ii) Tack the front neck facing pieces in position, right sides together as this will also help to prevent stretching.

(iii) Tack up, try on and make any necessary adjustments. Stitch up either the centre back or centre front seam.

(iv) Face the neck as described previously. Make a seam at the centre front in the same way as the shoulder joins. If zip is being inserted at centre front leave seam and facing unjoined.

(v) Top stitch neckline and centre front seam.

Preparing the tab

(i) Pattern

Size of paper $30\frac{1}{2} \times 7\frac{1}{2}$cm (12in. $\times$ 3in.). Draw a rectangle 20cm $\times$ $7\frac{1}{2}$cm (8in. $\times$ 3in.) and draw a

(5)   Pinafore tab

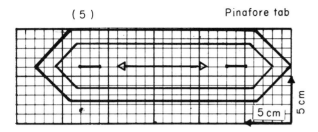

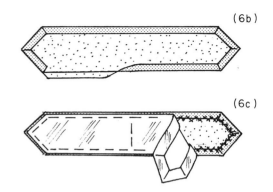

(6b)

(6c)

line parallel to, and midway between, the two longer sides. Extend the centre line by 4cm (1½in.) at each end and join to corners of rectangle to form points. Mark 1·5cm (⅝in.) turnings in, all round, within the tab (Fig. 5).

(ii) Cutting Out

Cut twice in fabric on straight grain, or, to reduce bulk cut one piece in lining. If using check fabric cut tab on cross for interesting effect (Fig. 6a).

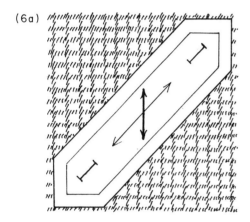

(6a)

(iii) Interfacing

Press firm iron-on Vilene to W.S. tab. Mark turnings.

(iv) Making Tab

The method described fastens the tab with Velcro. If you wish to make piped buttonholes instead, follow instructions on page 98.

Turn in 1·5cm (⅝in.) all round, tack and press. Trim raw edge to 6mm (¼in.) and cut away bulk at corners (Fig. 6b). If you have difficulty in getting a good shape at the ends cut a cardboard template from the pattern and lay this on as you tack.

(v)   These edges could be held down by slipping narrow pieces of Wundaweb under them, or if

you prefer, herringbone down.

(vi)   Remove tacks and press again.

(vii)   Place wrong side of lining to wrong side of tab. Baste up the centre to hold. Trim off 3mm (⅛in.) of the lining all round.

(viii)   Turn in edge of lining until it is 1½mm ($\frac{1}{16}$in.) back from edge of tab. Tack, press, hem all round (Fig. 6c).

(ix)   Remove tacks. Press again.

(x)   Mark position of button with chalk cross. Place tab in position on dress and baste up the centre. Do not pin or the tab will lift. Sew buttons at each end, without leaving a shank, through tab and garment, taking the stitches through the waist join where there is a double layer of fabric to take the strain (Fig. 7).

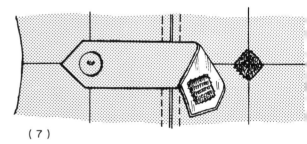

(7)

If you have inserted a centre front zip then sew the button through one end of the tab, sewing it flat with no shank.

At the other end cut a piece of Velcro to shape and hem in position. Sew button on top, flat with no shank. (Fig. 7.)

Imitation jetted or piped pocket

(i)   Mark position of pocket with chalk line adding two firm strokes across the end. Pocket can be any size but would not normally be more than 7½cm (3in.) long in this position.

(ii)   Cut a piece of fabric on the straight grain 2·5cm (1in.) wide and 20¼cm (8in.) long. Press Bondaweb to the wrong side using medium hot iron and damp muslin, waiting for it to become slightly speckled. After ten minutes, carefully peel off the paper.

Note: If using an even-check fabric for the tab and pocket cut this strip on the cross for an interesting effect.

(iii)   Fold strip in half and press, first with bare iron to ensure raw edges are level and strip is straight, then using damp muslin.

(iv)   Trim raw edge of strip. The width of this jetting or piping varies according to the fabric. For the materials suggested it should be trimmed to about 1cm (⅜in.) but if using a lighter fabric it could be less (Fig. 1a).

(v)   Cut strip in half, place one piece with cut edge against chalk mark and tack (Fig. 1b). Place other piece so that both cut edges are touching. Tack and then oversew the pipings together so that they do not part (Fig. 1c).

(vi)   Mark exact size of pocket on strips using tailor's chalk.

(vii)   Using a small machine stitch to lessen the risk of fraying, lower the needle into the centre of one strip, in the middle. Lower the foot and machine exactly in the middle of the strip as far as the chalk mark. Turn, with needle in work, machine to chalk mark at other end, turn and stitch back to the centre (Fig. 1d). Repeat on second strip.

(viii)   Remove from machine, cut off ends of thread.

(ix)   Turn to wrong side and cut pocket slit, exactly between rows of stitching. Cut long points at ends as shown and snip right to the machining (Fig. 1e).

(x)   Push strips through to wrong side, pull to flatten. Oversew edges of pipings together, tuck in triangles of fabric at each end (Fig. 1f).

(xi)   On wrong side, draw pipings together as far as end of buttonhole. Lift pipings and catch down the end triangles (Fig. 1g).

(xii)   Press, first from wrong side with medium hot iron, could be steam iron, then turn to right side and press again with light pressure and more steam either from the iron or from damp muslin.

(xiii)   Cut a piece of fabric on the straight grain 9cm (3½in.) long and 2·5cm (1in.) wide. Place it at the back of the pocket right side down. Tack in position. Oversew raw edges to raw edges of piping, all round, trimming it to fit and trimming off ends of piping if necessary. Press. (Fig. 1h.)

(1a)

(1b)

(1c)

(1d)

(1e)

(1f)

(1g)

(1h)

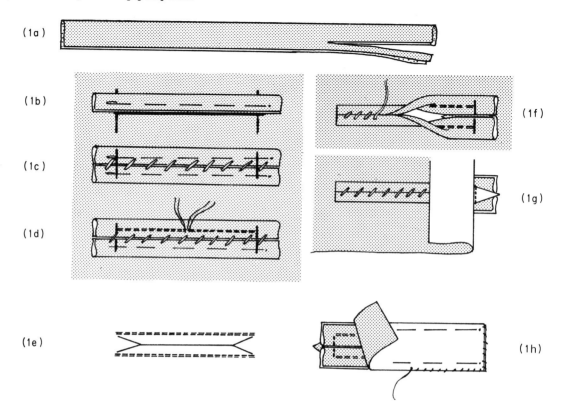

3
One-piece dress

Many people prefer a dress without a waistline because they find the line more flattering to their particular figure. Having fitted and altered the basic two piece dress pattern it can be converted into a one-piece. The bodice is used as it is, and the skirt added to it. The darts remain the same, so there is no additional fitting to be done in that area. The slit neckline is also retained as in the centre front seam. Later styles show the centre front cut to a fold.

The exact amount of ease required in a one-piece dress varies with size and figure type so it would be safest to cut out the first dress with 2·5cm (1in.) turnings at the side seams and fit it carefully to the figure, marking on the pattern any adjustments that need to be made.

Converting the basic pattern to one piece

Front
(i) Trace bodice onto a large sheet of paper, (approximately 125cm × 50cm (50in. × 20in.), omitting the turnings at waistline. Extend CF line 68·5cm (27in.) (63·5cm + 5cm (25in. + 2in.) for hem) or whatever length you require. At right angles to this, at the hemline, draw a guide line approximately 40·8cm (16in.) long.
(ii) Measure down from waistline 17·8cm (7in.), mark. Measure at right angles to this point $\frac{1}{4}$ hip measurement + 2·5cm (1in.) for ease and 1·5cm ($\frac{5}{8}$in.) seam allowance. Join to waist with a slight curve on side seam. Extend this line straight to hem line, giving added flare.

One piece dresses   As basic dress but no waist seam

One piece–dress; the pattern

(1)

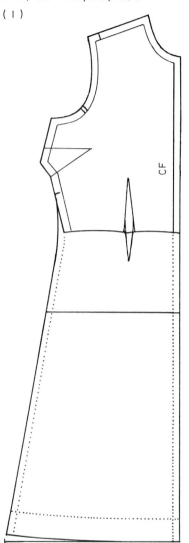
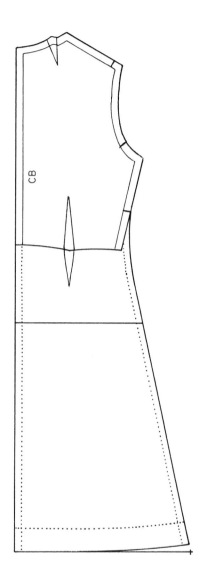

(iii)   Curve hemline by raising 1·5cm ($\frac{5}{8}$in.) at side seam.

(iv)   Dart: Extend dart below waist 6·7cm (2$\frac{3}{4}$in.) but reduce the width at the waist 0·6cm ($\frac{1}{4}$in.). Curve the sides of the dart slightly at the waistline so that it is not angled.

Back

(i)   Trace bodice onto a large sheet of paper. Extend CB line by the same amount as at CF and draw in guide line.

(ii)   Measure down from waistline 17·8cm (7in.), mark. Measure at right angles to this point $\frac{1}{4}$ hip measurement + 1·2cm ($\frac{1}{2}$in.) for ease and 1·5cm ($\frac{5}{8}$in.) seam allowance.

(iii)   Join, extend and raise hemline as given for front.

(iv)   Dart: Extend dart 10cm (4in.) below waist, but curve slightly below waist to reduce width and eliminate angles.

4

Day dress

Description

One piece dress, slightly A-line skirt, long cuffed
sleeve and roll collar. Alternative necklines:
shaped, stand collar, V-neck with braid trim, or
tie collar. Alternative sleeves: short or long and
fitted.

Fabric suggestions

All styles are suitable for any light or medium
jersey fabric including Crimplene, Trevira, Courtelle, wool. Featherweight clinging jersey would
hang well if mounted onto nylon jersey.

Contrasting fabrics in plain or print could be
used for the collars and cuffs.

Pressing

Use a steam iron over a damp muslin on the right
side or steam iron alone on wrong side. If using
an ordinary iron, place dry muslin on fabric then
damp muslin on top. When pressing seams or
other narrow ridges use light pressure and
immediately run the iron under the edge to
remove any marks. With acrylic jersey leave to
cool thoroughly before moving.

Haberdashery

5cm (22in.) nylon zip, 2·5cm (1in.) Velcro or two
small hooks for collared version, 2 reels Drima,
20cm ($\frac{1}{4}$yd) lightweight iron-on Vilene.

Figure types

Flattering to the shorter figure with thick or
short waist. Not for those with tiny waist and

One piece dresses.   CF cut to fold.
Roll or stand collar.
Fitted sleeve with cuff.

big hips or thighs. Avoid the high roll collar with a short neck.

Order of making up
(i)   Darts
(ii)   Centre back seam and zip
(iii)   Shoulder and side seams
(iv)   Collar
(v)   Sleeves
(vi)   Hem

Preparing a roll collar
(i) The Pattern
Size of paper: $40\frac{1}{2} \times 40\frac{1}{2}$cm (16in. × 16in.).
Draw a rectangle on the cross 45cm (18in.) long and 17·5cm (7in.) wide. Mark in 1·5cm ($\frac{5}{8}$in.) along one long edge. Mark straight grain. Cut out and mark the turnings along one side, mark the centre front (Fig. 1).
(ii)   Interfacing: the collar will roll better if a small piece of interfacing is inserted to support the neckline but the remainder is left soft.

Cut a piece of soft iron-on Vilene 3·8cm ($1\frac{1}{2}$in.) wide and 45cm (18in.) long. Press it to the edge of the collar that has been marked, on the wrong side. (Fig. 1.)

Preparing a long sleeve with cuff
(i)   The Pattern: shorten the basic long sleeve by 2·5cm (1in.) including the hem. Measure 10cm (4in.) up from the wrist curve to mark depth of cuff. Trace off. Mark in turnings all round, mark straight grain (Fig. 2).
(ii)   Cutting Out: cut out twice in fabric, four pieces in all, matching the straight grain. Mark

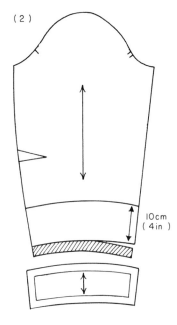

(2)

10cm
(4 in)

Sleeve with cuff

turnings on one pair.
(iii)   Interfacing: interface one pair with soft iron-on Vilene.

Double ended darts
Fold so that tailor tacks meet, and tailor tack marking the point is right on the fold. Place a few pins across the dart and one just beyond each end. Tack with small stitches.

After fitting, press the fold lightly, cut off the knot of the row of tacking and at the other end trim off the end of tacking thread. Machine in a

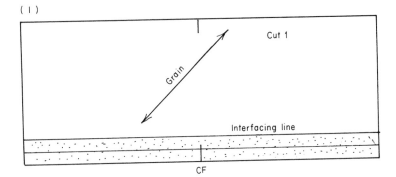

(1)

Cut 1

Grain

Interfacing line

CF

gradual curve from end to end. Work slowly to
avoid a drag on one side.

(4)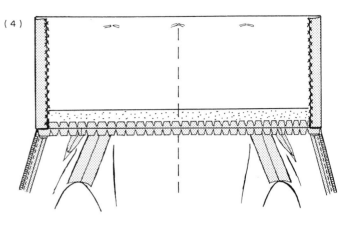

Remove tacks. Press stitching flat, snip into
centre of dart. Place on pad or sleeve board and
press as though it were two darts, working to one
point and then the other. Turn to right side and
press again protecting the work with a damp
cloth.

Attaching a Roll Collar

(i)   Place marked edge of collar to neckline of
dress, matching centre front lines, right sides
together (Fig. 3). Try to ease the collar rather

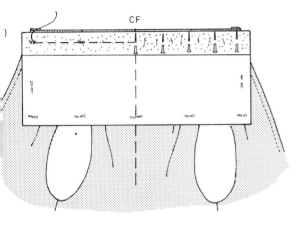

(5)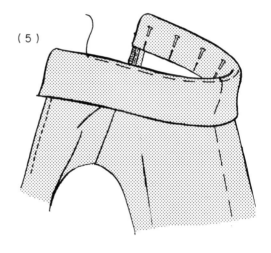

than stretch it. If a roll collar lifts in wear and
reveals the neck join it is because insufficient
ease has been allowed at this stage. To keep the
amount of ease even start pinning at the centre
front and work out to each end (Fig. 3).

(ii)   Trim down the turnings a little and snip at
intervals.

(iii)   Machine the neck join. Remove tacks, snip
turnings every ·6m ($\frac{1}{4}$in.) and press join open.

(iv)   Turn in the ends of the collar level with the
zip, tack press and herringbone down (Fig. 4).

(v)   Fold collar down so that raw edge covers
neck join. Pin and measure the amount the collar
is folded over. In order to make sure the collar is
an even depth turn to right side of garment, fold
collar edge over and tack, using a marker or tape.
(Fig. 5). On the inside tack the raw edge down.

(vi)   Slip stitch the ends and stab stitch through

(6)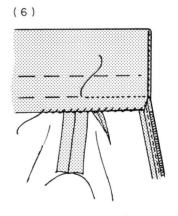

the neck join to hold collar down. Trim and neaten raw edge of collar (Fig. 6).

(vii)   Remove tacks from folded edge before pressing. Press the neck and ends well with a damp muslin but run the iron lightly along the fold of the collar edge stretching it slightly. While still warm roll the collar over into position and crease gently with your fingers, do not press.

Fastening collars at centre back

(i) With hooks and loops

Use two hooks size 0 or 00 and attach with button-hole stitch to the inside of the stand collar. Begin by anchoring the head of the hook slightly back from the edge, then sew with close stitches all round the two loop sections.

Work two small thread loops just inside the other edge making a bar with 4 or 5 strands of thread before covering them with loop stitch (Fig. 7).

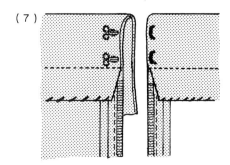

On a roll collar the hooks should go on the inside part of the collar but it is often also necessary to put at least one on the outer section as well.

(ii) Press stud

If fabric is very fine use a size 00 press stud, sewing the knob section under the edge of the right side of the collar, using buttonhole stitch but sewing the well section to the left edge just by firmly sewing through one hole, the remainder of the press stud being left to extend. When it is fastened the collar falls edge to edge (Fig. 8).

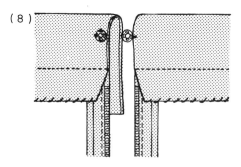

(iii) Velcro

This method is satisfactory for all collars that meet edge to edge and has the additional advantage of holding the collar upright. When using this on the roll collar note that the Velcro is stitched to the outer section, one piece extending (Fig. 9).

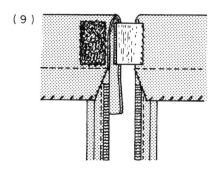

Making shaped cuff

(i)   Join ends of all 4 pieces. Trim. Press seams open (Fig. 10).

(ii)   Place pairs together right sides facing, tack and machine round top edge, making sure seams are matched. Trim down and snip.

(iii)   Turn to right side and roll edge, pulling interfaced piece underneath slightly. Tack and press (Fig. 11).

(iv)   Work a row of basting just below this edge.

(v)   Stitch and press dart and sleeve seam. Slip cuff onto right side of sleeve, matching the seams and with the interfaced section against the sleeve (Fig. 12a). Tack this layer only to the sleeve. Machine, trim, snip and press this seam open. Use a rolled towel or pressing pad to slip inside wrist (Fig. 12b).

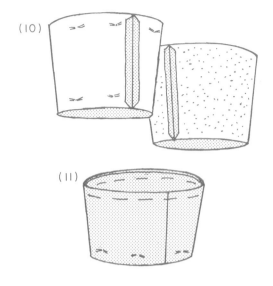

(10)

(11)

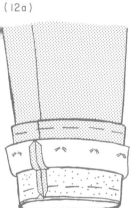

(12a)

(12b)

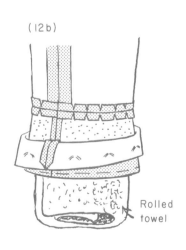

Rolled towel

(vi)   Fold cuff back into the position it will adopt in wear and baste along the roll to hold. Turn sleeve wrong side out and bring raw edge down to cover the seam (Fig. 13a). Be sure to keep cuff rolled back while doing this, tack, stab stitch through join, neaten raw edge. Press roll only lightly (Fig. 13b).

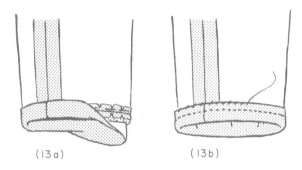

(13a)   (13b)

Preparing a stand collar

(i) The pattern. Size of paper 26 × 21 cm (10 × 8 in) Cut in squared paper as shown. Test it carefully against the neckline of the dress or pattern. Adjust the length at the centre back (Fig. 1).

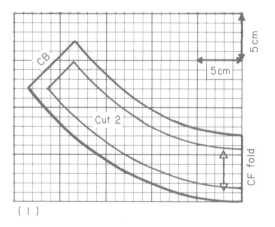

CB

5 cm

5 cm

Cut 2

CF fold

(1)

(ii) Cutting Out

Fold fabric on straight grain. Place CF pattern to fold. Cut out and tailor tack. Remove pattern and cut again, possibly in lining to reduce bulk, but there is no need to tailor tack this pair.

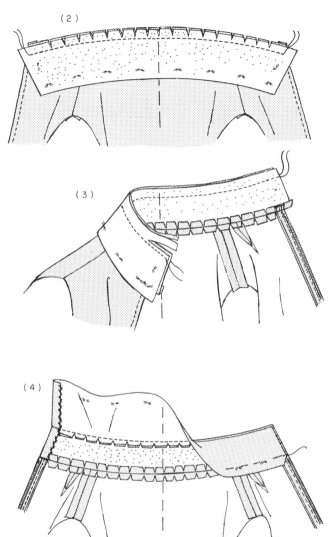

(iii) Interfacing
Interface the outer collar with firm iron-on Vilene.

Attaching the stand collar

(i)   Place collar right side down to right side of neckline, matching the centre front lines. Tack in place starting at the centre front. Snip the turnings of collar and neck if necessary. Machine. Remove tacks, press join open, snipping further to make it lie flat (Fig. 2).

(ii)   Place inside collar to outer collar, right sides together. Tack along top edge and machine. Trim and snip, trimming inner collar narrower than outer (Fig. 3).

(iii)   Press this join by placing seam over sleeve board or pressing pad and opening carefully with the toe of the iron. Do not try to press it right open, merely draw the iron along the join, then quickly press the turnings to one side, towards the outer collar. Turn work over and using a damp muslin press the right side too but only on the join or the rest of the colla can easily become creased.

(iv)   Roll inner collar over to wrong side and tack top edge, pulling join slightly to inside. Press. (Fig. 4.)

(v)   Turn in collar ends level with zip, trim, tack, press and herringbone down. Fold over and tack along neck (Fig. 4). Slip stitch collar ends, prick stitch along neck line through join working from wrong side. Neaten raw edge, snipping if necessary to allow it to lie flat. Press. (See Fig. 4.)

5

Braided V-neck dress with short sleeves

Use lightweight sew-in Vilene for the neckline. Prepare the pattern and then measure the neckline and sleeves to calculate the amount of braid required.

Preparation
(i) The pattern: use the one-piece dress pattern, mark the V-neck as described on page 110.
(ii) Cutting out: cut out a high neck to start with in case you find it too low. Tailor tack the neck and mark centre front.
(iii) Tacking: tack interfacing to the whole area of the front necks. Do not use the iron-on varieties as the pressing may stretch the neckline.

Fitting
Fit neckline carefully, mark new neckline if too low or too high. Place braid in position and decide how far from the neck edge to place it. Handle V-neck as described on page 110, inserting interfacing.

Attaching braid to V-neck
The position of the braid at the neck will depend on its width, but also on the effect you want to create.

The correct neckline and the centre front must be clearly marked. Using a marker or tape run a row of tacking round the neck where you want the inside edge of the braid to lie.

With the dress front on the table right side up, start at the centre front and tack braid in position

One piece dresses   V neck, short sleeves, braided

with the edge level with tacking. Work from centre front to shoulder one side and then from centre front to shoulder the other side (Fig. 1a). Do not add braid to back here.

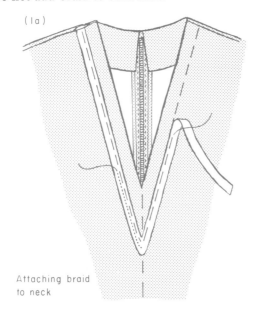

(1a)

Attaching braid
to neck

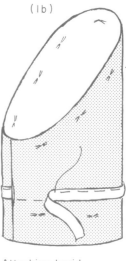

(1b)

Attaching braid
to sleeve

If possible, tack slightly off-centre or you may have difficulty in removing the stitches later.

A wide braid can be anchored with Wundaweb and the tacks removed before the permanent stitching is done. With some braid it will be possible to ease round the point without a mitre.

Stitching by hand
Use the same pricking stitch used for sewing in zips and other almost invisible work. Stitch down the centre, do not pull thread tight. At the shoulder sew the end down and neaten the raw end with a few overcasting stitches.

Stitching by machine
Put the quilting foot on the machine, which will enable you to watch the needle carefully. Set the stitch to a fairly large one and machine slowly up the centre of the braid, starting at the centre front and working up to the shoulders. Sew in the machine ends at centre front. Neaten ends of braid. Stitch shoulder seams and attach neck facings.

Attaching braid to sleeves
(i)   Stitch sleeve seams and turn up hems, tacking only the lower edge.
(ii)   Use marker or tape and place row of tacking round sleeve the same distance from the edge as on the neck.
(iii)   Tack braid in position (Fig. 1b). At under-arm seam, snip one machine stitch, push raw ends of braid through. Re-stitch the seam for an inch or so. Stitch braid in position by hand or machine making sure that the hem turning does not get caught in stitching. Finish sleeve hems.

If you particularly want to put braid round the back neck the same method can be used, i.e. joining shoulder seams and then snipping a stitch to push the ends through. However, it is difficult to re-stitch with the braid exactly accurate as it tends to slip, and whereas a very small movement will not show under the arms, it would look very bad on a shoulder. It is made more difficult at the shoulders too by the seam being sloping and the braid meeting at an angle.

Pressing
Try to avoid pressing on the braid on the right side, place right side down on to a towel and press lightly on the wrong side.

6

Making a curved belt in plain fabric

(i)   Lay your waist length of curved petersham on to a fairly heavy Vilene (this could be an iron-on variety, but test it first with your fabric).

(ii)   Mark round and cut out the Vilene but add 10cm (4in.) for fastening. Trim one end to a point if desired.

(iii)   Place the Vilene on a double layer of fabric and cut round allowing extra for turnings.

(iv)   Baste Vilene to wrong side of one piece and attach all round edge with herringbone stitch. If belt has point at one end make sure it will fasten right to left.

(v)   Place both pieces of fabric, right sides together, tack and machine along concave edge 2mm ($\frac{1}{16}$ in.) away from Vilene (Fig. 1).

(vi)   Run the toe of the iron along the join, pressing the turnings up into the belt.

(vii)   Roll the edge and tack.

(viii)   Turn in raw edge of fabric onto the Vilene, tack, trim away surplus and trim bulk in corners (Fig. 2).

(ix)   Press and catch down with herringbone stitch.

(x)   Bring backing down and baste through middle of belt to hold in position.

(xi)   Trim outer edge a little, turn raw edge under so that it is slightly back from the edge of the belt. Tack, press, and hem with very close

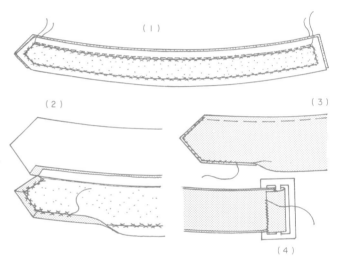

(1)

(2)

(3)

(4)

stitches (Fig. 3).

(xii)   Slip end through buckle, fold back and hem firmly in a rectangle (Fig. 4).

(xiii)   On the other end sew a 5cm (2in.) piece of the soft side of Velcro, cutting it to shape, but attaching at least 3mm ($\frac{1}{8}$in.) from the edge.

(xiv)   Try belt on over dress, mark position for second piece of Velcro. Before sewing on the hook side of Velcro trim off 1·3cm ($\frac{1}{2}$in.). This ensures that the rough side is always covered even if you adjust the belt.

7

Short skirt

Description
A-line skirt with side zip and inverted pleat at centre front and centre back. The waist is finished with petersham.

Fabric suggestion
Trevira/rayon, firm wool, Terylene, close knitted fabrics such as wool or synthetic jersey.

Pressing
Medium hot iron and damp muslin and plenty of firm pressure especially on the pleat.

Haberdashery
Waist length of curved petersham, 2 large hooks and eyes or 8 cm (3in.) Velcro fastener, 20cm (8in.) or 23 cm (9in.) concealed zip, 1 reel Drima.

Figures type
A classic style for any figure, but the pleats are particularly flattering to large thighs – balance your figure by choosing a top carefully to wear with it.

Order of making up
(i)   Pleat   (iv) Zip
(ii) Darts   (v)   Waist finish
(iii) Side seams   (vi) Hem

Fitting points
Any alterations you made to the skirt of the dress will still apply. In addition, when you try the skirt on you may need to tighten the waist by taking in the side seams. Find your exact waistline when you are ready to finish it by putting the skirt on, fastening the petersham round the waist on top, and chalking all round level with the top edge.

From basic skirt
with inverted pleat CF and CB.
Side zip

Pattern

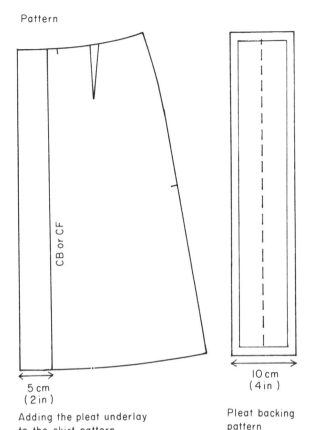

CB or CF

5 cm
(2 in)

Adding the pleat underlay
to the skirt pattern

10 cm
(4 in)

Pleat backing
pattern

Making up and attaching petersham

(i) For hook fastening. Turn back ends of petersham and hem or machine so that it fits your waist when the edges meet. For Velcro leave one end extending by 8cm (3in.).

(ii) Sew the hooks and eyes or Velcro in position.

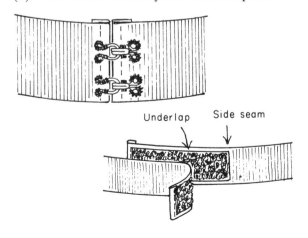

Underlap   Side seam

(iii) Turn in top edge of skirt, tack and press without stretching. Neaten the raw edge.

(iv) Place petersham inside top edge of skirt and with concave edge of petersham to the top of the skirt, pin so that petersham is just below the edge. Tack.

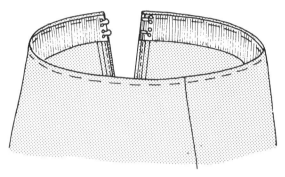

(v) Either machine from the right side using a very small zig-zag stitch, or hem by hand. Work a small bar tack beside the zip at each end to take the strain.

Inverted pleat

(i) After cutting out the skirt, tailor tack the centre front line. Shape the pleat edges and the pleat backing by trimming back 2·5cm (1in.) or so at the waist to reduce bulk.

(ii) Place the two front skirt sections together, right sides facing, and match the centre front lines carefully. Tack. Measure 15cm (6in.) down from waistline and put chalk mark to indicate top of pleat. This depth can be varied according to taste from 10cm (4in.) to about 20cm (8in.) but, if you have large hips, don't stitch it down too far.

(iii) With normal machine stitch, machine from the chalk line up the waist, fastening off the threads (Fig. 1). Adjust stitch to maximum length, lower needle into fabric exactly at the base of the first row of stitching and machine from there to the hem (Fig. 2). Do not fasten off ends.

(iv) Press stitching flat, then use the toe of the iron to open the pleat on the stitching line. Press pleat open firmly, using a damp muslin if necessary. The pleat is not finished at this stage but the

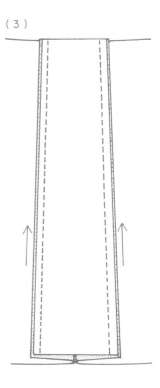

skirt is ready for a fitting. Make a chalk mark or put a pin on the right side level with the depth of pleat to show you at your fitting where the pleat ends.

(v)   After fitting, undo tacking in side seams and finish pleat.

(vi)   Lay skirt, wrong side up, on table. Place pleat backing on top, right side down. Match the centre, with the pleat line beneath and tack up the middle.

(vii)   Slide your hand under the two layers of pleat and lift slightly so that you can baste together from hem to waist. Finally tack the two edges together on the seam line.

(viii)   Machine the pleat edges together. Trim and neaten to within about 7·5cm (3in.) of the hemline (Fig. 3).

Turning up a hem with pleats in

(i)   Put the dress on and have the hem level marked with pleats still stitched in.

(ii)   Remove dress, run tacking thread round hemline but where pleat occurs work tailor tacks, penetrating all layers of fabric. As the tacks have to be snipped into three, leave long loops between the stitches. Part the three layers of fabric carefully, starting with the underneath one, and snip the tacks. (Fig. 4).

(iii)   Undo the row of big machine stitches holding the pleats in. This can often be done by grasping one end of the thread and gently easing the fabric along.

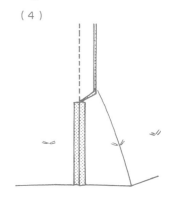

(iv)   Press open the pleat joins from the lower edges up to where the neatening ends. Trim the raw edges down to 3mm ($\frac{1}{8}$in.) for a non-fraying fabric, a little more for a fraying fabric.

(v)   Turn up the hem in the usual way all round the skirt, pressing and trimming down and neatening the raw edge. Catch the hem down as usual but at the pleat joins, snip the raw edges in towards the seam and then stitch the hem down.

(vi)   Lift up the raw edges and complete the neatening, working round the corner at the bottom to finish off.

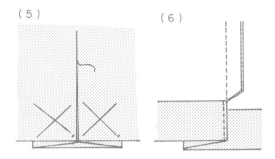

(5)　　　　　　　　(6)

Stitching pleats to prevent them opening

Fold the pleat into position and tack with a double diagonal stitch (Fig. 5). Turn to the wrong side and stitch from just inside the bottom up to the hem edge, sewing near the edge through all layers. This can be done by machine if you can keep your stitching straight through this thickness (Fig. 6), but it is often easier to back stitch by hand.

Press the hem in the usual way and re-press the pleat edges but as you have uneven layers of fabric, pad the board with a towel first as it is easy to finish up with pleat backing imprints showing in the hem.

8

Long skirt

Description
Long skirt with deep frill at hem, which could be a contrasting fabric. For a more sophisticated line omit frill and cut longer.

Fabric suggestions
Bold printed synthetics, fine wool, synthetic crêpe. Plain version without frill could be velvet, velveteen, brocade, lurex jersey, cloque.

Pressing
Steam-iron for lightweight synthetics and wool. Dry-iron only on brocades. To press velvet and other pile fabrics place a piece of spare fabric pile side up on the pressing board. Place section of garment pile downwards and press very lightly using a medium-hot iron and damp muslin. Hang up to cool.

Haberdashery
Waist length of petersham or waistbanding, 20cm or 22cm (8in. or 9in.) concealed zip, Wundaweb for hem, 2 spools Drima.

Figure types
In the right fabric and with the right top this is right for anyone. In large print for slim hips only. Wear with plain dark top to disguise a large bust, or make skirt in dark fabric and top in print to disguise large hips.

Order of making up
(i) Tack darts and side seams and fit. Finish

Long skirt with frill
or plain floor-length
Side zip

darts and seams.

(ii)   Zip.

(iii)   Waistband.

(iv)   Attach frill. Fold frill and press (or turn hem if single).

(v)   Tack up hem of skirt and tack to frill.

(vi)   Fit length.

(vii)   Remove frill and finish hem of skirt (Wundaweb).

(viii)   Attach frill to skirt.

Fitting

Frill is 20cm (8in.) deep finished; if you need to shorten the skirt take some off the skirt edge where it joins the frill to keep to this depth. If making a plain skirt add 20cm to skirt length before cutting out.

Preparation

Use skirt pattern as shown on p. 127 but lengthen, allowing 2·5cm (1in.) hem if attaching frill or 5cm (2in.) if making plain. Cut off seam allowances at centre front and centre back and cut to fold (Fig. 1).

Make waistband as described on page 127.

Cutting out the frill

Cut lengths of fabric on the straight grain 45cm (18in.) wide and join until you have a piece double the length of the distance round the bottom of the

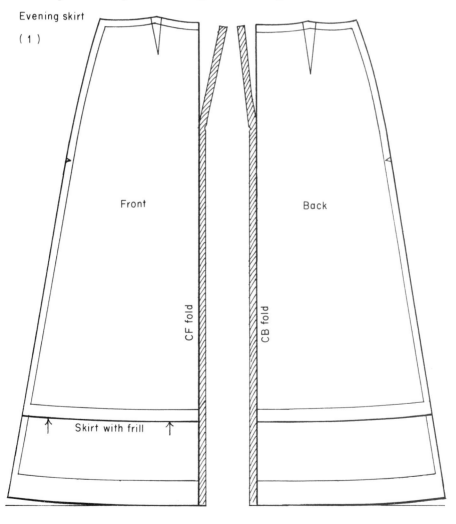

Evening skirt

(1)

Front

CF fold

Skirt with frill

Back

CB fold

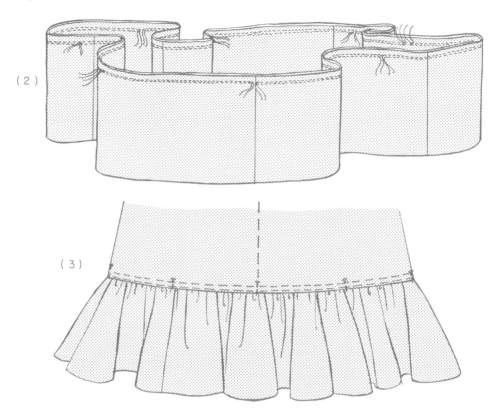

skirt. If the fabric is too stiff or bulky to make a double frill then cut the same length but 25cm (10in.) wide.

Making and attaching the frill

(i)   Join frill into continuous piece, trim and press all joins. Fold and press.

(ii)   Insert threads for gathering in raw edge, stitching through both layers. Put in short gathering threads in case one should break when pulling up, dividing the frill up into 8 sections and insert 2 gathering threads in each (Fig. 2).

(iii)   Turn up the lower edge of the skirt 2·5cm (1in.) and tack. Divide hem evenly into 8 sections. Pin skirt to frill at these points and draw up gathering threads until each section fits the skirt. Wind threads round pins to hold. Tack skirt to frill and try on for length.

Remove frill from skirt but leave gathers pulled up. Adjust hem of skirt if necessary then finish by neatening the raw edge and either slipping Wundaweb under it or catch-stitching it down.

Lap skirt edge over frill, pin the 8 sections again, evening out the gathers. Tack twice, once on the fold and again 1·3cm ($\frac{1}{2}$in.) in. Machine with a medium-length stitch from the right side, with thread that blends in with the print, this will not necessarily be the background colour of the print. Work two rows of machining 1·3cm ($\frac{1}{2}$in.) apart. Neaten raw edge of frill on wrong side (Fig. 3).

Plain skirt

For the skirt without the frill simply turn up the hem and finish in the usual way.

9

Evening dress

Description

Short or long evening dress from one-piece pattern. Scooped neckline, beading optional, waist decoration. Sleeveless or could have long fitted sleeve from dress on p. 117.

Fabric suggestions

Plain moss crêpe, satin, slub weave rayon or silk.

Pressing

Use very light pressure and the toe of the iron; take care not to let double edge cause ridges. Use steam iron on wrong side only for difficult parts, but whichever method is used, move the iron quickly or the fabric may shine. Do not use any moisture or steam on pure silk.

Haberdashery

55cm (22in.) nylon zip, 20cm ($\frac{1}{4}$yd) soft Vilene, 10cm ($\frac{1}{8}$yd) firm Vilene for belt, 1 button, beads or sequins.

Figure types

This is very slimming at the waistline as the area of waist is broken by the small belt. Flattering to the rectangular or thick-waisted figure.

Order of making up

(i)   Fit darts but make up and insert belt in front darts before machining.
(ii)   Insert interfacing in neckline cut to same shape as facing.

One piece dresses.   Boat neck
tie or tabs above waistline
sleeveless or longsleeve

(iii)   Finish zip, shoulder seams and side seams.
(iv)   Attach facings to neck edge and join shoulders but do not trim or roll the edge until beading or embroidery has been worked.
(v)   Work beading or embroidery through fabric and interfacing.
(vi)   Complete neck facing.
(vii)   Finish armhole edge with facing or insert long sleeves.
(viii)   Turn up hem.

Preparation

(i) The pattern

Use the one-piece dress pattern and lengthen if desired. Cut a scooped neckline on the front and back bodice of the one-piece pattern (Fig. 1). Remove seam allowance from centre front and mark 'Cut to Fold'. The scoop neck is 6·5cm (2·5in.) wider at the shoulder and 2·5cm (1in.) lower at centre front. If you habitually suffer from

(1)

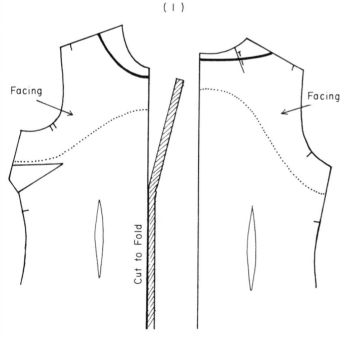

gaping at the front on low necks, then also take 13mm (½in.) off the neck edge of the centre front, to reduce the width. Run this off to nothing at bottom of pattern. On the back bodice lower the

neckline 1·3cm (½in.) at the centre, although this could be lower if you prefer. Pin out the back neck dart before cutting the new neckline. The back dart is still there but shorter. Add turnings to neck edge before cutting off.

Cut all-in-one armhole facings as described on page 136.

(ii) Cutting out

If you are unsure of the depth of neckline or it is the first time you have tried the style, cut out to the normal round neck but tailor tack the new lower one and check it at fitting.

(iii) Interfacing

Interface neckline with soft Vilene using the facing pattern as a guide. This means you will be interfacing right across to the armhole but it will help support the embroidery and also prevent underarm creasing which is often a problem with evening dress fabrics.

Fitting points

(i)   Check width of neckline.
(ii)   Establish position of belt, if you are short waisted, place it fairly low, if an Empire-line suits you then place it quite high.

Inset belts

(i) The Patterns
Size of paper: Tab 15cm × 5½cm (6in. × 3in.)
                     Tie 25½cm × 12½cm (10in. × 5in.)
Cut patterns as shown, mark straight grain. Do not cut the shaped end of the tab, leave pattern as rectangle.
(ii) Cutting Out
(a)   Tab: Cut a piece of fabric 7·5cm (3in.) wide and 60cm (24in.) long, (or two pieces each 30cm (12in.) long) cut in half across the middle and interface one piece. Cut this into two and also cut the other piece, thus giving you 4 pieces (Figs. 2&3).
(b)   Tie: Cut pattern out twice in fabric.
(iii) Interfacing
Use a firm weight iron-on Vilene in the tab and a soft sew-in variety in the tie. Try out the iron-on Vilene on a scrap of fabric first to make sure it

Pinafore tie and tab

(2)

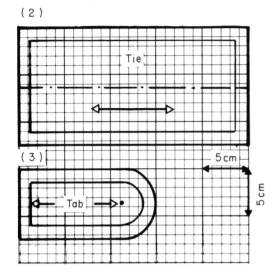

does not show. If it does, use a firm sew-in variety.

Tab belt

Place pieces together in pairs right sides facing, baste. Trim turnings off pattern and lay on fabric, matching straight grain exactly. Tack round edge of pattern, holding the layers together (Fig. 4).

Before machining, chalk round the end to provide a guide for stitching.

After machining, trim and layer the turnings and snip. If the fabric frays, anchor a small piece of Wundaweb in the end of the non-interfaced side. Turn through, roll edges. Tack and press.

Protect the fabric with a dry cloth when pressing the right side. Lap one piece over the other and sew button right through both layers.

(4)

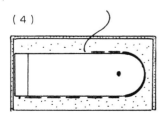

Tie belt

Fold each piece in half, right side inside, and machine the raw edges together. Trim and press seam open with toe of iron. Bring seam to centre and machine across ends (Fig. 5). Cut in half to make two pieces; turn each one inside out, tack and press. Insert in dart as described next.

(5)

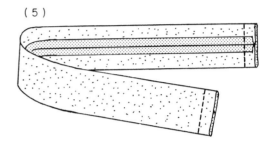

Inserting the belt

After fitting the darts and marking the position, split the fold of the dart on the wrong side and snip the tacks. Pass belt through, centring button over centre front line of dress. Make sure belt is level by measuring to the top of each dart (Figs. 6a&b).

Machine darts, neaten raw edges.

Inserting belt

(6a)

(6b)

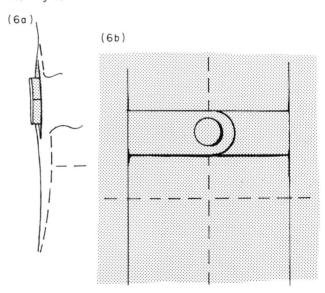

(7)

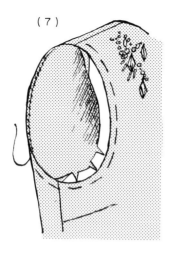

Finishing neck and armhole facings

(i)   Trim snip and roll neck edge. Tack and press lightly.

(ii)   Join underarm seams on facings.

(iii)   Neaten raw edge of facing.

(iv)   For sleeveless dress turn in seam allowance and tack snipping as necessary. Press. Turn in facing seam allowance, snipping where necessary and tack down. Hem all round (Fig. 7).

(v)   If inserting sleeves baste armhole edges of dress and facing together and set in the sleeves.

10

Long dress with trumpet sleeves

Description
A one piece dress with full trumpet sleeve edged with wide bias strip in matching or contrasting fabric. Use the one piece dress pattern lengthened to floor length.

Fabric suggestion
Brocade, silk, velvet, synthetics such as Tricel, heavy cotton etc.

Pressing
Press according to the fabric but set the sleeves in last to avoid crushing.

Haberdashery
55cm (22in.) zip, 2 Reels Drima, soft Vilene for neckline, contrasting fabric if desired for sleeves.

Figure types
This type of sleeve is at its fullest at hip level and should be avoided by pear-shaped figures.

Order of making up
1 Follow order for basic dress
2 Make up sleeves
3 Set in sleeves
4 Hem

Fitting
Any alterations made to the basic pattern will apply to this sleeve.

One piece dresses.   Wide sleeve and binding
Neck facing applied to outside

Long dress with trumpet sleeve.
One piece dress – (no waist seam, no CF seam)

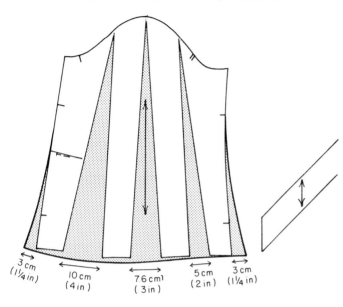

3 cm
(1¼ in)   10 cm   7.6 cm¹   5 cm   3 cm
            (4 in)   (3 in)   (2 in) (1¼ in)

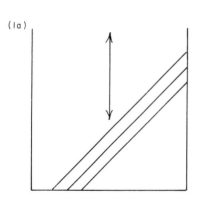

(1a)

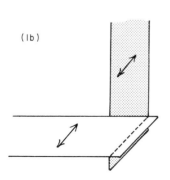

(1b)

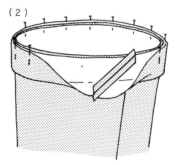

(2)

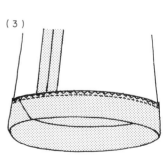

(3)

Preparation

(i) Pattern

Cut 2cm (¾in.) off the lower edge of the sleeve pattern. Cut the pattern into 4 and fold out the elbow dart. Spread out the pieces and insert extra paper as follows: 10cm (4in.) in the back in line, 7·6cm (3in.) in the centre and 5cm (2in.) in the front. In addition, shape the side edges out in a curve to a point 3cm (1¼in.) beyond the original position. Curve the bottom of the sleeve. Mark straight grain down centre of sleeve.

(ii) Cutting Out

Cut the sleeve on double fabric matching up the straight grain.

Bias finish

(i)   Cut 2 crossway strips 6cm (2½in.) wide on the bias of the fabric, each long enough to go round the bottom of each sleeve (Fig. 1a). Join the strips if necessary, with the joins on the straight grain (Fig. 1b).

(ii)   Fold strips in half lengthwise and press with wrong sides together.

(iii)   Pin, folded, round base of sleeve, matching raw edges and with strip to right side sleeve. Make the join line up with the underarm seam (Fig. 2).

Stitch and press the join, then tack the bias strip to the sleeve.

(iv)   Machine, taking 1cm (¼in.) turnings.

(v)   Trim the raw edge a little and neaten either with a small zig-zag stitch or by hand overcasting (Fig. 3).

11

Dress with full sleeves

Description

The basic dress with long full sleeve gathered into a wrap cuff and fastened with a small piece of Velcro.

Fabric suggestion

Any soft or crisp fabric but nothing bulky: featherweight Crimplene or other synthetic jersey, Viyella, brushed rayon, linen-look, polyester/cotton.

Pressing

Press according to fabric. Press sleeves before attaching cuff and then take care not to crush them in handling.

Haberdashery

55cm (22in.) zip, 2 Reels Drima, light or medium weight Vilene for neckline and cuffs, 5cm (2in.) Velcro fastener 20mm wide or 10cm (4in.) Velcro 11mm wide.

Figures types

Almost anyone can wear the basic dress and the full sleeve adds interest.

Order of making up

(i)   Making up basic dress as before.
(ii) Make up sleeves and cuffs.
(iii) Set in sleeves.
(iv) Hem.

Basic dress.   As basic but long with full sleeve into wrap cuff. Shaped belt optional

Fitting

Any alteration to the length of the basic sleeve will still apply to this sleeve.

Preparation

(i) Pattern

Cut basic sleeve pattern into 4, fold out the dart and spread out on new paper inserting additional paper for fullness only at the wrist. Insert 7·5cm (3in.) in the back slit in line with the little finger, insert 5cm (2in.) in the centre slit and insert 2·5cm (1in.) in the front in line with the thumb. Curve bottom edge, dropping it slightly at the back (Fig. 1). Mark the straight grain down the centre of the sleeve.

Note that the sleeve pattern is left full length and the cuff is additional. This gives an attractive puff to the sleeve.

For the cuff pattern, draw a rectangle the size of your wrist plus 2·5cm (1in.) long and 12cm (4½in.) wide. Add turnings all round. Mark straight grain down centre.

(ii) Cutting Out

Cut out the sleeve and cuff on the correct grain on double fabric. Mark all turnings.

(iii) Interfacing

Interface wrong side of cuffs with iron-on or sew-in Vilene.

Wrap cuff

(i)   Insert two gathering threads round the lower edge of the sleeve. Set your machine to the largest stitch that it will do, start well inside the edge to keep away from the underarm seam and reverse for a few stitches, then machine to the same point at the other side of the sleeve. Do not reverse or fasten off. Work with right side of work uppermost.

(ii)   Place cuff to sleeve right sides together, pin at each end, pull up gathers to fit. Pull up only the spool thread, i.e. the one on the wrong side of fabric and wind the end round a pin to hold. Even out the gathers and tack. Machine.

(iii)   Trim turnings and press down into cuff.

(iv)   Fold sleeve right sides together and tack and machine the seam through the sleeve and through the cuff. Keep the cuff joins level by

inserting a pin and stitching over it.

(v)   Turn in raw edge of cuff and tack to row of machining. Hem.

Attaching Velcro

Try sleeve on and mark wrap over in line with your little finger. Cut the Velcro in half lengthwise if using the wide one, and hem the pieces in place so that when fastened it fits your wrist.

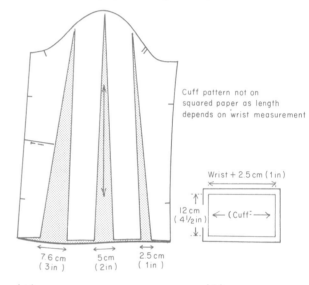

Dress with full sleeves gathered into wrap cuff – Basic dress shape (waist seam, CF seam)

Cuff pattern not on squared paper as length depends on wrist measurement

Wrist + 2.5 cm (1 in)

12 cm (4½ in)   ← (Cuff) →

7.6 cm (3 in)   5 cm (2 in)   2.5 cm (1 in)

(1)

(2)

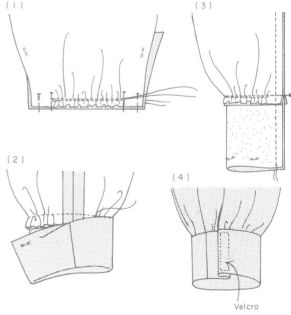

(3)

(4)

Velcro

Index